READING CHAMPIONS!

Second Edition

TEACHING READING MADE EASY!

READING SUCCESS RECIPES
FROM 500+ CLASSROOMS

Rita M. Wirtz, MA

LifeRich Publishing is a registered trademark of The Reader's Digest Association, Inc.

LifeRich Publishing books may be ordered through booksellers or by contacting:

LifeRich Publishing
1663 Liberty Drive
Bloomington, IN 47403
www.liferichpublishing.com
844-686-9607

ISBN: 978-1-4897-3396-2 (sc)
ISBN: 978-1-4897-3397-9 (e)

Library of Congress Control Number: 2021903373

Print information available on the last page.

LifeRich Publishing rev. date: 02/25/2021

Acknowledgments and Dedication

When others want us to be successful, there is no greater gift. I am truly blessed by such support. Many people have been in the village of my life encouraging and helping me complete this book.

To start with, thanking my family and friends; you met some in my Memoir, Vicki, Shirley, Ellen, Judith, Brooke, Casey. Over the years, good friends mean a lot.

I have a large tight knit family, including my sister Sheryl and brother-in-law Rick. Also, Rebecca, Kristin, Heidi, Stephen, Danya, Jim and their kids. Five grandchildren. Nephews: Michael, Steve and Ted. Nieces: Katrina, Beth, Rita. Erinne and cousins, you are in my thoughts and heart.

To my other Eugene family, Max and Monica Linhardt, Harper. Sam, my inspiration and constant support whether doing needed tech work, advising, motivating and telling me from the start I could do this. Sam's patience, tenacity, common sense, is always invaluable. To find a partner so late in life was an unbelievable gift.

To those angels watching over me, I know your light surrounds me. Remembering my parents who encouraged me to be a reader and teacher, plus adored husband William, brother Marshall, dear friends, Pam Laird and Estelle Werve.

To Don Werve for believing and assisting for many years, offering editorial ideas, adding Linguistic feature to "Reading Champs" and always believing in me.

To Tom and Cheryl Thien, preschool directors, thanks for mentoring me, and being part of our family. Teaching young children brand new reading skills is such a joy; watching you with kids, a once in a lifetime experience.

To staff of Bell Avenue School. You made dreams come true and years later what we did still shines brightly. Jeanette Kajka, Paula Weiss, my Robla District and Bell Avenue teacher friends, special thanks for keeping me connected.

To Rebecca Clements, of LifeRich for encouraging me, and helping me be a successful author during challenging times.

To Robin Tappan for time, expertise and belief in this book, offering production-advice, motivation and creative presence.

To Hal Powers, author, for listening and coaching me about my unique writing style and helping me polish art and craft.

To all the schools, children, parents, educators I met along the way, it's hard to believe I am still here, doing 'my thing' after fifty years. You made it happen.

To my colleagues on social media, especially Twitter, my gratitude. Inviting me for special appearances on podcasts, video- casts, teacher chats, and so much more. Being a lifelong learner has been such an important part of my life as teacher.

Although a totally consuming project, so many people urged me toward the finish line, it's impossible to list everyone here, but know I appreciate your contributions.

Overcoming great obstacles, due to the pandemic, I am thrilled to present Volume Two of my flagship book "Reading Champions". It means so much to me that I could do this. It seems like such a miracle. I am especially grateful to my daughter Rebecca, son-in-law TJ and granddaughter, Morgan for always encouraging me!

Sometimes it takes just a word or two to change a life, or maybe validate your thoughts. I fervently hope my words and lessons have the power of belief, magic of unicorns, and the beauty of rainbows. May you continue helping kiddos become capable, confident readers who love to read!

To Tyler Trostrud, technology expert and editor, you made this happen. My gratitude!

Leaving footprints on your reading hearts, Rita

EPIGRAPH

"All I Really Need To Know I Learned in Kindergarten (Uncommon Thoughts on Common Things"). By Robert Fulghum, 1986.

This book has always meant a lot to me. Sometimes little things are big things. My last classroom teaching experience was in preschool, which surprisingly, turned out to be one of the most extraordinary learning experiences in my life. Let's think about this.

"All I really need to know how to live and what do and how to be I learned in Kindergarten. Wisdom was not at the top of the graduate -school mountain but there in the sandpile at Sunday School. These are the things I learned:

Share everything. Play fair. Don't hit people. Put things back where you found them. Clean up your own mess. Don't take things that aren't yours. Say you're sorry when you hurt somebody. Wash your hands before you eat. Flush. Warm cookies and cold milk are good for you. Live a balanced life - learn some and think some and draw and paint and sing and dance and play and work every day some. Take a nap every afternoon. When you go out into the world, watch out for

traffic, hold hands, and stick together. Be aware of wonder. Remember the little seed in the Styrofoam cup. The roots go down and the plant goes up and nobody really knows how or why, but we are all like that. Goldfish and hamsters and white mice and even the little seed in the Styrofoam cup- they all die. So do we. And then remember the Dick and Jane books and the first word you learned- the biggest word of all— Look."

PREFACE- Backstory

Everything in my career has been rewarding, but probably the most significant was making "Housecalls" to nearly six hundred classrooms, engaging in action research and modeling reading strategies. It's always good to "walk the talk", then "talk the walk".

I lived a crazy schedule during those years, teaching University courses in Reading and School Administration Monday nights, sometimes two nights a week, then traveling another three or four days not only in California, but across the United States, alternating Seminars, with Keynotes, classroom work and writing.

I kept stacks of letters from kids and their teachers, and other tangible memories. The rest, always in my heart. I have no regrets about being a helper. I always felt I was destined to do this. I still feel that way. As of January 2021, I have been an educator, teaching one level, one way or another for fifty years.

I can't even imagine when I say that, but I always believe experience counts. At this life and career stage I am "passing the torch". I believe it's important I share what tricks of the trade I know. Why should these strategies sit on my shelf? Sometimes one idea sparks an aha moment.

During those years, for over a decade, I was privileged to teach for and with thousands of educators and parents. Sometimes I stayed with Principals and teachers I met along the way. Even now, I am fast friends with a number of people from way back, and that says and means the world to me.

Those who can, teach. "Reading Champions" was my gift in 2002 to a myriad of educators at schoolhouse and home. After I left each session of "Housecalls" I was asked by teachers to share what we had discovered worked with their classes.

So I developed some sort of framework or graphic organizer, etc. I wrote on scraps of paper, napkins, backs of envelopes and finally started bringing my laptop with me, along with a training trunk overflowing with Seminar Books, give-aways, samples, gifts for teachers and their classes. When I arrived at my hotel room for the night, I wrote. Finally, I had a book!

Continued...

My dear colleague and friend Shirley Willadsen and others from San Diego

County Office of Education put together a major program with me, for "Reading Champions." First, I taught (trained") a cadre of leaders developing their reading programs. I was actively making "Housecalls" to their classrooms at that time, and co-teaching with their Teachers and Principals. While at each school site, I generally met with families, modeling easy to do at home, reading practice activities, too.

San Diego County Instructional TV Department filmed me teaching classes, unrehearsed up on a stage and in a Kindergarten classroom. Ultimately we ended up with three videos, two matching guidebooks, and the master "Reading Champions" book ('02, Volume 1).

Kathleen Bulloch, Executive Board of California ASCD (Association for Supervision and Curriculum Development) wrote a Book Guide for this master book, along with my Introduction; you'll find this at the Addendum. This brief Reading Guide may be used as a preview of the chapters or after, as reflective action.

In any event, realizing everybody's a reading teacher now, I decided to release this old friend, my flagship book. Out of print for so long, I followed this book with a number of other articles and books, culminating in "Reading Champs, Teaching Reading Made Easy", and then "Stories From a Teacher's Heart", a Memoir.

I decided to offer Volume Two of my original "Reading Champions" because it's so needed now. I have always specialized in foundational reading skills, nuts and

bolts. Common sense, fast, fun and highly effective strategies make a big difference in engaging all learners to become capable, confident readers who love to read.

I hope you enjoy skimming and dipping in to what you're most interested in. This isn't a cover-to-cover read. Discover quick tips, builders and boosters, shortcuts and interventions and most of all, build your confidence as you explore what works, a step by step approach for successfully instructing fundamentals of reading to readers of all ages and stages. Enjoy the reading celebration!

INTRODUCTION

In this book you learn...

1. Teach Your Students What Good Readers Do

Discover how to turn your students into strategic readers through direct explicit instruction, modeling, guided and independent practice.... Teach students to have a purpose for reading, use their background knowledge, make connections, predictions, adjust rate to purpose and monitor their comprehension.... Find out what good readers do to decode and understand new words, read actively and extensively.

2. Learn How to Make Decoding Instruction More Effective

Practice a variety of multi-sensory ways to teach word recognition and structural analysis.... Learn how to teach the fundamentals in small, manageable steps through practice.... Discover time-tested, research based strategies which fill in the gaps and make an important difference in your teaching.... Master basic reading skills instruction.

3. Explore the Systematic Phonics Sequence and How to Teach It

Regardless of the grade level you teach, all students need to know how to decode unknown words. Fill in the gaps using these ready-to-go mini-lessons which teach or review essential vowels and variants, consonants, blends, digraphs, diphthongs and word family patterns.... Practice effective ways to review contractions, syllables, compound words, prefixes and suffixes..... Get practical suggestions for enhancing current techniques.

4. Build Vocabulary Through Direct Instruction Activities

Discover unique ways to improve your direct instruction of vocabulary, including review of word parts such as prefixes and suffixes, using word origins, context cues and glossaries.... Explore ready-to-use vocabulary boosters including graphic organizers, charts, spelling rules and extension activities.

5. Discover How to Enhance Fluency and Vary Rate

Use time-tested techniques which help your students become more fluent readers whether reading silently or orally... Discover how to help your challenged learners read out loud with confidence, appropriate speed, accuracy and expression.... Find out how to use repeated readings, tracking strategies, skimming, scanning and visual/perceptual activities.

6. Learn Effective Comprehension Strategies for Expository Texts

Help students make better sense of expository texts through a prescribed sequence.... Learn how to make use of prior knowledge, form accurate predictions, ask questions and summarize.... Discover effective pre and post reading techniques.... Find out how to easily teach the structural features of textbooks....Help students understand difficult textual material.... Motivate students to want to read textbooks and non-fiction.

7. Enhance Comprehension of Narrative Material

You receive quick tips for teaching fiction.... Encourage students to read chapter books and novels in addition to anthologies.... Instill the love of literature as the heart of your reading program.... Quick and easy ways to review the basics, including plot, characters, setting, theme and story grammar.... Modeling reading a variety of genres.

8. Discover Time-Tested Shortcuts, Corrections and Interventions

Best of all, here are prescriptions for reducing or eliminating common "miscues"- reading errors and difficulties including reversals, problems with directionality and tracking, losing one's place, eye teaming problems, sub-vocalization, fixations and regressions.

9. Find Out How to Accelerate Progress of Really Challenged Readers

Review the Mechanics of Reading.... Learn when to refer.... Discover when to intervene with modifications or interventions and what type.... Find out how to flexibly group way below level readers....... Tips for helping second language learners master basic reading skills.... Rethink the concepts of readability and leveling..... .
Master "double alignment", matching curriculum, instruction and assessment to your students and state standards.

10. Learn Exciting Ways to Involve Parents With At-Home Reading

Include parents in interesting ways which make a genuine difference.... Connect with real-world reading, parents will enjoy doing with their children.... Enhance the school-home literacy partnership.... Help parents understand how they can motivate their children to read.

What Do I Know Already?

What Do I Want to Know?

HOW TO USE THIS BOOK

1. Decide your purpose for reading this book.

2. Connect this book with other material you have read about teaching reading (if any), and your background knowledge. (Schema)

3. Do KWLW (Know and Want to Know) parts.

4. Make predictions what this book will be about.

5. Do a Book Walk. Read 9 Big Ideas, 12 Success Secrets, Table of Contents, etc. Use your current preview strategies.

6. Skim this whole book. Dip into sections (chunks) you're interested in, and want to learn more about.

7. Read, skim, dip in as much of the book as possible in each study session.

8. Confirm your predictions. Make new ones as you go.

9. Use one chunk (section/part) at a time.

10. Apply the strategies. Do the mini-lessons.

11. Practice the new techniques every day, in short sessions.

12. For building new vocabulary, start a list or word bank, or make flash-cards to study and remember.

13. Do KWLW (Learned and Want to Know Now) parts. What do you want to learn more about?

There is no one best way to teach reading, so get set for a review of the fundamentals. This is not a reading program, these strategies complement whatever program you are already using. Get out your document camera, smart board and get started!

12 TOP NOTCH READING SUCCESS RECIPES

Favorite Catch Up or Go Ahead Strategies.

Success Secret #1
Know the Reading Process, in Brief

Success Secret #2
Know the Mechanics of Reading

Success Secret #3
Teach Basic Phonics

Success Secret #4
Teach Easy Start Decoding Sequence

Success Secret #5
Teach Structural Analysis

Success Secret #6
Correct Common Errors and Difficulties

Success Secret #7
Model Lots of Vocabulary Word Play

Success Secret #8
Teach Students to Spell New Words Correctly

Success Secret #9
Review Basic English Grammar

Success Secret #10
Teach (Model) What Reading Champions Do

Success Secret #11
Teach Comprehension (Non-Fiction) Fundamentals

Success Secret #12
Teach Core Literature Classic Fiction

NINE KEYS TO CREATING READING CHAMPIONS

Nine BIG IDEAS Are Chapters In This Book!

1.   Set the Stage to Create Success.

2.   Easy Start Mini-Lesson Planning.

3.   Basic Reading Success Recipes.

4.   Teach Structural Analysis.

5.   Reading Shortcuts and Interventions.

6.   Word Slingers (Vocabulary Builders and Boosters). Spellers, too!

7.   How Reading Champions Read Non-Fiction.

8.   Easy Start Memory Joggers.

9.   How Reading Champions Read Fiction.

Want to Learn ONE More Thing?
Selected Resources & More.

CONTENTS

NINE BIG IDEAS IN THIS BOOK

P.S. Want To Learn at least ONE More Thing?

Chapter 1

Set the Stage to Create Success

Striving for Excellence Starts Here ...

This chapter helps you make an important difference in your classroom or learning environment. By carefully considering the fundamental information reviewed here, you will more quickly and easily help your students meet state standards. We need to rethink some prevailing practices which may or may not be getting good results. This chapter assists standards-based lesson planning. Best of all... motivate yourself to help "at promise" kids, succeed.

Introduction or Rationale
Balance Your Program
Use High Interest Materials
Motivate Your Students to Read
and more ...

INTRODUCTION TO CHAPTER 1

"We tend to teach the way we are.
Not everyone learns like us."
Rita Wirtz

In this first section of **Reading Champions!** you learn basic tips for getting started or revamping your reading instruction. There is a solid review of things to "revisit" as you initiate lesson plans which help students master essential skills measured by standardized assessments as well as everyday anecdotal information. Reading research now advocates going beyond a balanced literacy program. Teachers need to have a wide knowledge of supportive reading practices which help ensure diverse learners become capable, confident readers. Today, currently a pendulum swing to "Science of Reading" moves us back to code first, phonics. Balanced Literacy always included code and meaning. Reading is brain based, definitely. Cueing, which I still use as one of many strategies, is not in favor, certainly not as a stand alone technique.

Balance your reading instruction
Set up a basic skills curriculum
Create a print- rich environment
Motivate kids to read

BALANCE YOUR READING PROGRAM

1. Print and language rich environment
2. Reading to students
3. Modeling reading strategies
4. Language experience
5. Directed reading lessons
6. Independent reading
7. Writing
8. Basic Skills
9. Spelling
10. Speaking and listening

SET THE STAGE TO CREATE SUCCESS!

Include in Your Curriculum

1. Abundant reading, time to read
2. Book "conventions" (concepts of print)*
3. Phonics review, fundamentals
4. Strategies for self-monitoring*
5. Vocabulary
6. Comprehension
7. Study Skills
8. Rate builders
9. Spelling
10. Writing

* Concepts about print include book conventions, letters have meaning, spacing as function, directionality and tracking, punctuation, upper and lower case letters, etc.

CREATE A PRINT-RICH ENVIRONMENT

In your language-rich classroom all types of print are displayed. This includes Environmental Print, Functional Print, and Dramatic Play Print. Display print on walls, doors, bulletin boards, cabinets, clothesline, etc. Make and use *Word Walls*.

(Depending on age and level of student.)   (Depending on age and level of student.)

1. Environmental Print–Signs and print in our environment— initial stage of reading. In your classroom:

    - Play print games such as Bingo, Tic-Tac-Toe, Dominoes, board games, etc.
    - Application forms (Samples.)
    - Wall areas covered with environmental print. Drivers' license practice book pages, etc.
    - Sample contracts

2. Functional Print–This type of print provides information. In your classroom, this might be:

    - Charts: sign in, attendance, lunch schedule, etc.
    - Good morning message or assignment
    - Center Rotation
    - "How To" charts, such as steps to writing process, etc.

    THOUGHTS & IDEAS:

3. Dramatic Play Print– reading, writing, language involved in these activities:

    - Role play
    - Simulations
    - Reader's Theatre
    - Plays
    - Creative Dramatics

4. Book Nook: What's in a Book Nook?

    - Books! (books face out).
    - Check-out system
    - Rocker/Couch/Bean Bag/Carpet/ Rug/ Pillow/ Chair
    - Bathtub/Tee Pee
    - Reading posters
    - Writing and drawing materials

5   Student Work–Post less commercial and more student work (correct models). Change daily or weekly to keep current.

USE HIGH INTEREST READING MATERIALS

You can really reach kids when you use "stuff" they're interested in.

For example:

1. Internet or other articles about interesting topics.

2. Use magazines, graphic novels, read-alongs, etc. that are especially appealing to kids. John Dewey taught us that interests are important.

3. If students don't like to read, check out picture books, graphic novels and favorite classics. Mix it up. That just right book makes a difference.

4. Current novels and stories with an edge, contemporary, mixed in with classics work great for the balance.

5. Provide real life reading practice with newspapers, drivers license book, contracts, things that are important to kids. "Realia" or "actuals", real life stuff.

6. Cartoon books, comic books, joke books provide opportunities to review phonics, and teach comprehension tips.

7. Environmental print is important. Signs and maps offer useful practice.

8. Ask students what they want to read. An Interest Inventory works well, but just asking the kids provides enough and best information. Meeting interests first works to grab kids' attention.

3 R's: Risk + Repertoire = Results

Balance

The reading program should be balanced with a combination of textbooks, if they are used, internet resources, core literature classic novels, and high interest materials. Ensure students learn ready-to-use strategies applicable to any info-text material (non-fiction). Fiction may include junior novels, core literature and sufficient titles to make an impact. Aim for study of at least one novel per month for skill levels 3-9. I still favor whole class novels. High interest materials might be fiction, non-fiction, or a combination of numerous kinds of print.

MOTIVATE YOUR STUDENTS TO READ

Interest+   Need to Know+

Right Stuff to Read+

Using Skills+   Concentration=

READING CHAMPIONS

1. Interest is the key to all reading. When students are interested, they pay attention, focus, and concentrate.

2. Need to know provides the structure and format of the reading experience. For most students, there is a big difference between want to read and need to read.

3. Right stuff to read considers the balanced reading program. And, what do students want to read? A wide variety of genres (types), textbooks and methodology should be included. Reading should be at an independent or instructional level. Always avoid study at the frustration level.

4. Using skills is critical. Skills must be practiced every day. Mini-lessons are a great way to teach for the first time, or review missing skills, and fill in the gaps. Mini-lessons are short chunks, or pieces one skill at a time, 5–20 minutes.

5. Concentration is easy when students are interested and have a need to know. Emotional involvement, novelty, and prior knowledge of the subject are important factors.

Thoughts and Ideas:

GROUPING TIPS

(All Skill Levels)

Avoid "ability grouping" Use Flexible Grouping.
Focus on what skills do students have or lack?

Flexibly group for brief skill-based mini-lessons daily, or as possible. Make it informal, but keep track of progress. Running records or other assessment tools you are using now are fine. Whatever you need or want to use works for me..

Whenever teachers say to me, "Rita, I have a very low class this year." I say, "Great, what a wonderful challenge. I wonder what it will take to get good results with this group?" We need to plan based on skills known and unknown to meet students' individual needs and differences. Equity.

This book is filled with ready-to-use, time-tested, skill-based mini-lessons in decoding, vocabulary, spelling, reading fiction & non-fiction, comprehension, and rate builders. All activities work as teacher-led direct instruction, small group mini-lessons, and individualized practice. Schoolhouse and home.

Regardless of current skill level, set a reading goal for everyone, including the teacher (and family).

Reading better, faster, and more, is *ongoing* and *lifelong*.

THE CONTINUUM: A NEW SLANT

STUDENTS:

Learn to Read (K-2 Skill Levels)

Read to Learn (3-6 Skill Levels)

Learn to Read more and better (7-Adult)

Every student should have a reading improvement goal, regardless of how well he she thinks they read currently.

Parents and teachers should also have goals. The faster students read, the better their comprehension.

Teach students to vary rate according to purpose for reading. When reading for information, not every word has to be read. Go for big ideas.

Read!

FINAL COMMENTS: CHAPTER 1

BEAT THE ODDS

STRIVE FOR EXCELLENCE
Create Reading Champions!

Believe:

1. All kids are potential geniuses, regardless of past experience.

2. Kids are "At-Promise," not "At-Risk."

3. To boost self-esteem, build basic skills.

4. There is no such thing as failure, only feedback.

5. Kids are doing the best they can, with the resources they have. They are perfect in every way.

6. It's not what they do, it's how we *react* to it.

7. Many kids are "disaffected" —they see no purpose, relevance or meaning in *school* or reading.

8. We need to speak their real world "language," to get genuine rapport.

9. To teach what *you* want, find out what *they* want and need to know. (What is it that they want to know?)

10. To promote learning—*Model* everything; provide a need to know, make it interesting, unusual, novel, exciting. Have fun with it.

11. "Practice makes permanent."

Repeat. Repeat. Repeat.

12. You can get and keep their attention!

Do:

1. Motivate kids.

2. Keep yourself motivated.

3. Treat yourself; take care of yourself.

4. Think positively, all day, every day.

5. Set big & small goals. Mark incremental progress.

6. Speak (learn) their language.

7. Find an "edge," and *use* it.

8. Make instruction truly meaningful.

9. Remember your sense of humor.

10. Use positive language. Avoid negative words.

11. Change your posture–change your attitude.

12. *Model* learning/studying.

13. Give choices. "You can do a, b, or c." Kids love choices.

Many of these ideas are based on the study of excellence, NLP, Neurolinguistics. I'm actually certified in both NLP and Hypnosis.

> ***Reading Champion Credo*:**
> Work hard!
> Take risks!
> Learn something new every day!

Chapter 2

EASY START MINI-LESSON PLANNING

"Practice makes the learning stick."
Rita Wirtz

This chapter assists with (standards- based) lesson planning. It is important to rʳthink some of the important factors for delivering quality direct instruction in mini-lessons or whole class, as well as making sure students are focused and ready to learn. Lesson design is an art form with distinct elements including the *set, or* opener, the body, complete with brain-compatible strategies, the *close* and critical transitions as well as practice strategies. Teaching the fundamentals becomes much easier in a strategic framework. **Skills** can be taught in chunks, or mini- lessons lasting between five to twenty minutes; whole class, small group or one- to- one tutoring work well, depending on benchmarks and assessment information.

Think It- Plan It- Teach It- Check It
Pay Attention: Get Ready to Read
Follow Directions
Surefire Sets
Colossal Closes
Get Results
ME! Model Everything

INTRODUCTION TO CHAPTER 2
HOW TO CREATE READING CHAMPIONS!

My favorite theme to tie a lot of classroom work to, is Heroes and Sheroes" (Heroines). Everyday heroes the students can relate to, surround us. Nearly daily there is something positive to use as a base for, or addition to, the regular lesson. I believe in using a lot of student choice, with students as designers of their own learning, teacher more as a sideline coach.

Motivate students constantly to be the best they can be, and assure them that they have great brains and are potential geniuses. To teach them, reach them first, matching what they want and need to know. Consider the constructivist viewpoint, if there is no meaning, there is no learning.

Celebrate what they can do, and already know. To build self-esteem, build skills. Instead of thinking about slow, or poor readers, consider what skills are known and unknown. Attach all new learnings to a "hook", and engage as many emotions as possible. Robert Sylwester once said "Emotion drives attention, attention drives learning." That has always stuck with me.

The set or opening piece of the lesson must be interesting, thoughtful, stimulating or exciting to create enough genuine interest to learn. Why do you need to know this? As a lot of students have short attention spans (think rapid-paced video games), teach your lessons in very short chunks, generally no more than twenty minutes per chunk. (A block schedule of ninety minutes has three to five chunks). This is why mini-lessons work!

Considering Primacy—Recency* theory, make sure every lesson or chunk of a lesson has a strong set, close, and a very fast paced but interesting middle portion.

This is called "elaborative rehearsal' strategies. I always recommend to teach (model) everything at least three times, in three ways. Offer lots of practice with oral choral response, and hands-on experiences.

Do mini-lessons daily. Use flexible grouping, moving students together per skill gaps, not perceived ability. Regroup daily, or throughout the day for skill work.

*Originator unknown, but widely known theory means students remember best what they hear first and last.

Everything is skill based and worthwhile to teach. There should be no fluff. Cut the junk, pare it all down to the briefest essence.

Teach only the fundamentals, using high quality strategies that teach students thinking processes involved (metacognition). No crossword puzzles, nonsense words, scrambled words, word searches, or fill-in-the-blank only worksheets. Use only correct models. Have students keep learning logs, and do continuous journal writing in all content areas.

Classrooms should be print rich and language rich as possible. Constant word play, grammar practice, language, listening and speaking activities. Every student needs to have a copy of content area textbooks, if in use. Core literature classic novels and high interest books should be full class set. I still advocate teaching whole class novels.

Teach only the fundamentals.
Use high quality strategies.

To accelerate or catch students up, use the following strategies outlined in this book:

1. Directed Reading Activities (DRAs)
2. Mini-Lessons of all types
3. Shortcuts and Interventions
4. Decoding Reviews
5. Vocabulary Builders
6. Rate (speed) Exercises
7. Visual and Perceptual Warm-ups
8. Comprehension Boosters
9. Study Techniques

GET THE READING RESULTS YOU WANT!

EASY START LESSON PLANNING

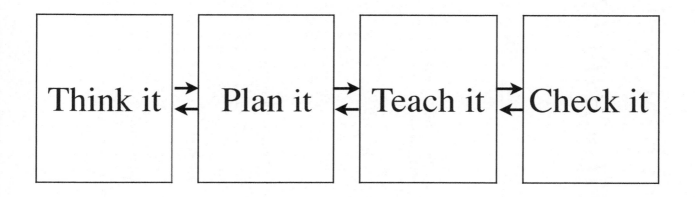

EASY START SKILLS TEACHING

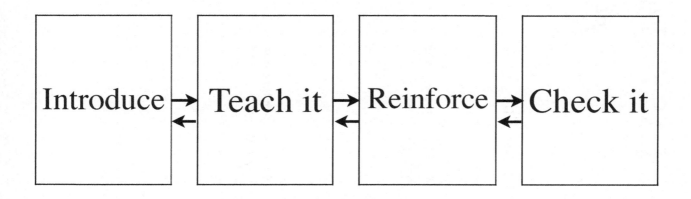

EASY START READING LESSON PLAN FORMAT

THINK IT-PLAN IT-TEACH IT-CHECK IT

Lesson Title _____ Standard _____ Date _____

1. What is the lesson about? (Subject matter)	2. What do they already know? (Prior knowledge)	3. What will they learn? (Objectives)	4. What to gather? (Materials & Resources)
5. How much time will This take?	6. Strategies to use?	7. Lesson chunks Set: Middle: Close: Extension:	8. Did it work? Did they learn it? What's next?

PAY ATTENTION: GET READY TO READ!

Turn on turned-off students fast (Get Their Attention!)

I think students should physically move, or at least stretch every twenty minutes in order to oxygenate the brain and return to a ready-to-learn state. Holding a stuffie or little ball might help concentration.

Warm Up Ideas/Brain Breaks/ Transitions

- Aerobic Moves (Set to music!)
- Climb Stairs (Pretend)
- Seal of Approval (Like a seal)
- Pat on the Back (Pat your back)
- Round of Applause (Clap in circle)
- Give a big hand (put hand out in front).

- Simon Says Game
- Pick apples, $100 bills (Reach up for)
- Snap-Sizzle (Finger snap, sizzle sound and movement)
- Train Wheels Rolling (Move and sound like a train)
- Wash Windows (Pretend)
- Hug yourself (You deserve it)
- Melt milk chocolate, butter (Pretend)
- *Brain Gym* movements
- Breathing! Breathe deeply
- Stretching! (With or without music)
- *I Feel Good!* (Shake it out!)

- Chair Aerobics (Use only your fingers)
- Popcorn! (Pop up like ..)
- Be Loose Like Spaghetti (Wiggle around like noodles)
- Bean Bag/Ball Toss (Koosh ball is great)
- Cheers! Hip/Hip/Hooray! (Make up cheers)

- Do tongue twisters
- Play music of varying types

TIP: use novelty to get students' attention. Things which are unusual stand out and are remembered.

PAY ATTENTION*
Concentrate and Focus.
Clear your mind (Repeat or Count 1-20)
Relax your body; breathe deeply Play Baroque music
Drink water
Use good posture
Get Interested
Organize Information
Preview -Read -Review
Use Study Strategies

PAY ATTENTION!

1. Concentrate—Focus

2. Clear Your Mind (Repeat or Count 1-20)

3. Relax Your Body; Breathe

4. Play Baroque Music

5. Drink Water

6. Use Good Posture

7. Get Interested

8. Organize Information

9. Preview - Read - Review

10. Use Study Strategies

FOLLOW DIRECTIONS

To teach students to follow directions, do the following:

1. Model what you want students to do, first. Have them go through the process, or the steps, with you.

2. Tell them what you want them to do. Break it into small chunks, easy to remember and do.

3. Write the steps up on the board or a classroom Anchor chart.

4. Use a large sized Sequence chart (with the steps visually represented.

5. Have students repeat back the directions to you, or in partners or small groups.

6. Make sure students are paying attention before you begin to give the instructions. Say, in a direct manner, with a commanding voice: "Listen to me now, this is important." Or, "Stop what you are doing now, and pay attention." Or, "You need to hear this. Listen!"

7. Use an auditory signal to get attention before you begin the directions, such as a loud bell, train whistle, etc. Visual signals (such as a blinking light) are lost on auditory and tactile-kinesthetic (predominant) learners.

8. Post a correctly headed paper online or Anchor chart, and leave it up there.

9. Have students (buddies) check on each other to make sure they are doing it the right way.

It's important to allow sufficient time to teach the routines of following a set of particular directions. There is a process or strategy of following directions; listening is one of the four components of literacy—reading, writing, speaking, listening. To ensure directions are understood, add in the visual— and the tactile-kinesthetic— the modeling and practice of each step. Practice following directions as a mini-lesson, as often as needed, until it is rote and transfers to students' study habits as an often used strategy.

USE SETS: 20 SUREFIRE SETS

It makes sense that students pay attention when they are motivated and/or curious about a subject. Ensure your subject is worthwhile and the lesson consists of meaningful, authentic activities. Be sure to answer "WIIFM What's in it for me?" every time, every lesson. "Why we need to know this."
Here are some of my favorite classroom-tested ways to kick off reading lessons, units, themes, or mini-lessons. Always SET everything you teach. It's often the key to success.

1. Meet students' needs, interests and aspirations—personalize it.

2. Add novelty to surprise and excite—props, sound effects.

3. Start with the global, or big picture, for overall understanding. Then the parts.

4. Connect to prior learning (Schema), recent or the past.

5. Tell students why it is important to study this.

6. Establish expectations for their learning. (What to know?)

7. Turn on appropriate background music to set the mood, to match the subject.

8. Tell a joke, story, metaphor, analogy or anecdote to provide interest and make a point.

9. Wear a special apron, hat, or costume. (Stuff from home.)

10. Rap the opening or sing the Set. Be outrageous and fun.

11. Brainstorm the opener.

12. Mind Map or Sketch Note the Set. (Margulies, Buzan, Jensen, etc.)

13. Model the learning first. Then kids do it.

14. Start with an illustration or diagram of some sort.

15. Kick-off with a simulation or role-play, to get in the mood.

16. Play a game, of some type.

17. Create a real-life problem to solve, right at the beginning.

18. Arouse curiosity by starting "What if..." And then get going.

19. Review what you've learned before in class, to make a connection.

20. Do KWLW, to build or connect with Schema, (prior knowledge). Do the KW parts of the KWL chart (Smart board or on paper, etc.)

How long? My sets vary from thirty seconds, to a whole lesson, as a set piece.

* Teach Big, piece, piece, Big.

USE CLOSES: 26 COLOSSAL CLOSES

DO THESE TEACHER FAVORITES:

Hint: Always close every lesson, unit, theme, or mini-lesson.

1. Quick mini two person debates (simulta-neous debates; partners switch sides). With brief review, students pair up, and take sides of an issue studied in class.
2. Caption a cartoon about the learning.
3. Think Ink Speak or Pair Share (or "Turn to your partner, and...)
4. Fish Bowl—selected students sit in a circle within or in front of the class (two circles) with discussion participants in the inner circle, teacher prompts discus-sion, 'audience' asks questions. After each round, switch circles.
5. Hot Seat—students respond to questions in the 'Hot Seat'. Team response.
6. Extension of Lesson—meaningful homework.
7. Once Upon A Time—tell a story about the learning. Around the class, or circle.
8. Pass The Microphone—pass around a 'toy' echo microphone—students share their favorite part of the new learning.
9. 'Sort and Store' Process—students share aloud or on paper what they have learned. ("I learned that. Now I want to learn," etc.).
10. Graphic Organizers, of varying types. Mind Maps. Sketch notes.
11. Write It Down—Tell your class to write down one to three things learned.
12. Learning Log or Journal Write. (Quick Write.)
13. Build A Model—tactile/kinesthetic way to show learning. Use tinker toys, tape, paper, straws, clay, silly putty, legos, any model building junk materials you have available. Maker space type activities.
14. Tea Party—students write one thing they have learned on an index card or piece of scrap paper. They rotate through the room, around the whole class, sharing.
15. Poem—write a poem about the content studied (must be at least three to four lines or more).
16. Alone or with a partner, or small group, write a rap, song, cheer, tune about the new learning. Make and write a haiku.
17. Make a Collage about the new learning.
18. Games to review the learning.
19. Dear...—write a letter to someone about the learning. Call on volunteer(s) to read their letter or pairs read to each other.
20. Ticket To Leave—Pass out a ticket to each student. Tell class to write down their favorite new learning and leave it on the way out of class. (Roll of pre-printed tickets or plain index cards.)
21. History Makers—identify a famous person in history. Have students (in groups or pairs) discuss how the famous person would approach, apply or think about the subject matter, and what they might say to you. Act it out out.
22. Winners—students select their favorite new idea or ideas, and provide rationale for their 'winner'. Students may make trophies, ribbons, etc. for their ideas.
23. Quilt It—students make a construction paper (felt or fabric square) quilt of their favorite concept learned. Piece together into a wall hanging.
24. Museum—create a hands-on project for a classroom museum.
25. 1-2-3 Know It. In groups of 3's or 4's: (Student 1 says one favorite thing learned or remembered. Student 2 repeats what 1 said, then adds one thing. Student 3 repeats what 1 & 2 said, then adds 1 thing. Class repeats, then adds their own favorite thing learned.
26. It's about—tell another student what you just learned, in one minute or less. Rotate through the class. Use frequently for a great, quick oral review.

GET GREAT RESULTS
WITH YOUR READING MINI-LESSONS

1. CHUNK the learning into teaching pieces.

2. KEEP UP THE PACE with lots of things to do.

3. ALWAYS SET AND CLOSE each chunk, each part of the lesson.

4. DO CLEAR TRANSITIONS between content pieces.

5. Sometimes REPEAT and REPEAT! Repetition makes the learning stick.

6. TEACH YOUR LESSON AT LEAST THREE WAYS. Better, students design their learning.

7. MODEL EVERYTHING and always use correct models.

8. USE BLOOM'S TAXONOMY as a basis for your planning.

9. Most of your lesson should be ACTIVE LEARNING; students are knowledge workers.

10. Allow enough time for PLENTY OF PRACTICE.

FINAL COMMENT: CHAPTER 2

The Very Best Reading Strategy Ever

ME

Model Everything!

Always Model everything in more than one way, and repeat it. Over and over. Overlearn it.

"Practice makes the learning stick."

Rita Wirtz

Chapter 3
Basic Reading Success Recipes
Focusing on reading instruction

An extraordinary review of reading research by the National Reading Panel documented in its summary and subgroups reports proven ways to improve the reading skills of American schoolchildren.

The National Reading Panel (National Institute for Literacy) delineated five major areas of reading instruction necessary to "leave no child behind". These include: phonemic awareness, phonics, fluency, vocabulary and text comprehension. Most state standards correlate with the NRP topics: word analysis, fluency, vocabulary development, comprehension, literary response and analysis.

This chapter assists with comprehensive insight, reliable information and effective strategies which help students master the fundamentals of reading. Moreover, the following classroom tested strategies are ready to go, which is an important factor for increasingly busy teachers.

Shortcuts and Interventions
Ready-to-Use Mini-Lessons
Know the Mechanics of
Reading Practice Tracking
Skills to Master
Teach Basic Phonics
Review the Decoding Sequence
Phonemic Awareness
Word Families
and more ...

INTRODUCTION TO CHAPTER 3

THE READING PROCESS, IN BRIEF

1. Students learn to manipulate the sounds in words. Phonemic awareness means students can play with the phonemes, basic units of speech that make up words. Reading researchers state the importance of this first skill as a strong predictor of reading achievement.

2. Students begin in a print awareness stage. They recognize that thought can be written, they look at print—the letters, the spaces between words. They understand how to handle books; they recognize what a word is.

3. Students begin to understand syllables and parts of words. Teach them to use onsets (beginnings) and rimes (endings) (word families) to recognize new words.

4. Usually consonant sounds are taught first, with alphabet recognition necessary to give a name to a sound (teaching vowels simultaneously or shortly after, to make words.)

5. Students must have a variety of strategies to monitor' or self-correct as they read. The three reading cueing systems may offer assistance to the reader.

6. The goal of reading instruction is to move a reader from a state of dependence to independence. When the student becomes fluent, this stage is called automaticity. This means that the decoding process becomes automatic, so that the reader has more time to comprehend in lieu of figuring out what a word is.

7. To nurture vocabulary, use rich oral language, direct vocabulary instruction and lots of exposure through wide reading. Students learn 2000-4000 words per year.

8. Building comprehension means that readers predict, understand and remember what they read. To do this, they need to be taught specific strategies which build comprehension. Readers must be actively involved in the reading process.

9. To become literate, students need to read widely, and constantly. Surround them with print. They need to be read to and experience the joy of reading. When they become fluent, and the reading is automatic, they are confident.

10. Learning to read is a lifelong process, along a continuum.

> *Thinking about what you just read,
> what are implications for your instruction?*

KNOW THE MECHANICS OF READING

DEFINE READING:

HOW I LEARNED TO READ:

Major Factors of Reading—Quick Overview
1. Physical (Also see Get Physical, Part 2)
   Eye Stop—when reading, eyes stop briefly (fixation) and then move to an-other stop. That is where recognition occurs. The reader's eyes take in the letters, in order. They actually see every letter, although as readers become more fluent it is an automatic process.
   Eye Span—amount of type seen in each stop. Visual/perceptual practice can assist the reader to see more in each stop.
   Regressions—the habit of (involuntarily) going back over material already read. Limit the number of regressions through tracking practice.*
   Vocalizing—sounding words—sub, or below the breath, vocalizing is usually word by word reading and may slow the reader down. Increasing the rate, increasing eye span and decreasing eye stops may eliminate sub-vocalizing. However, many auditory learners repeat or sound out the words and say to themselves.

2. Psychological
   Attitude/Motivation—Students who are successful readers love to read and find meaning in what they read. Build skills and model joy of reading.

3. Neurological
   Reading is brain-based. Thus, Science of Reading.

* Tracking means following along a line of print.

READING MECHANICS: GET PHYSICAL
EYES AND READING

A student may have 20/20 vision, yet have visual and perceptual problems interfering with reading.

Here's what to be aware of:

WHAT	WATCH FOR	DO
Eye Movement	Losing place, missing words, eyes jumping around. Rereads. Writes up or downhill.	Tracking practice; use finger or card as pointer. Use pacing device.
Eye Teaming	Squinting, covers one eye, blinking, lack of depth perception, poor spatial orientation. Sees double.	Brain Gym exercises (See Resources list).
Eye-Hand Coordination	Problems discriminating size, location of objects. (Small children–inability to stay within lines) Crooked writing. Left to right confusion.	Get physical—play jacks, "spear" cheerios, string beads, juggle, catch a ball, etc.
Visual Perception	Reversals, inability to use perceptual information such as shape, size, location, and distance. Confuses words. Likeness/difference.	See section on remediation of common errors and difficulties.
Observe, then refer	Appearance of eyes, eye complaints when reading, tension, headaches, etc.	Refer to optometrist.

Note: Optometrists may provide helpful advice regarding any visual/perceptual issues, and offer effective eye exercises.

EYE MOVEMENT IN READING:

FIXATIONS, REGRESSIONS

You may notice some students move their heads rather than their eyes, from left to right. The following information about eye movements in reading helps you make sense of students' head and eye movements.

A reader's eyes pause to focus on a group of symbols, move forward again, then move to the next symbols across the written page. This physical part of reading is called a "fixation".

Watch your students when they read; the number of words per stop is called the reader's eye span. Eye muscles are capable of seeing more print; more efficient readers have longer eye spans.

When readers look backward to fixate again on something they've already read, these are called "regressions". You may observe students regressing back to other words in a line of print, or paragraph. Too many regressions impair fluency (automaticity) and comprehension.

Some students may make as many regressions as fixations! To accelerate these students' reading, your goals are to widen the span, decrease the number of fixations, and shorten the time of fixations.

When teachers understand students' eyes actually do not move continuously along a line of type, the importance of visual and perceptual practice is apparent. Rate building is important, also.

DIRECTIONALITY

(K–1 Skill Levels, or gaps)

Directionality is critical to reading-following the print

Activities:

- 'L'—Show students the 'L' on the left hand (made by thumb and index finger).

- Simon Says ("Touch your right foot," etc.)

- Flashlight Walking—Have a student hold a flashlight in each hand. He/she takes a step with right foot and says "right." (The flashlight is beamed at the right foot). Do left next and repeat.

- Brain Gym— Works well!

- Sorting Games—Right and left gloves, shoes, placing items in pockets, or jars, etc.

- Up/Down/Below—Use movement for body concepts. Have student show you with his/her body up, down, over, under, etc. Climb over things, under, etc.

- Give Directions—Use directions with whole body movement such as "get behind John", "sit in the seat to the right of my desk," etc. Act it out.

- Draw a map on the floor, using chalk or masking tape, string or ropes. (oops-no masking tape on carpet).

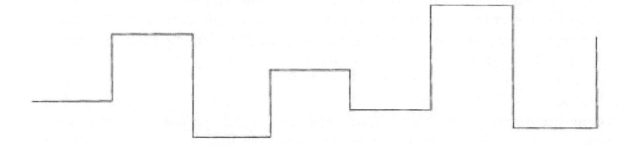

- Have a student walk through the classroom map and at each corner, state which direction he/she needs to go, before turning. Say it out loud.

- Have students mark and draw on paper as you give the directions: the right, left, bottom, etc.

PRACTICE TRACKING

(K–6 Skill Levels, or gaps)

All kids need to do or review tracking-following lines of print

1. On a given line of type have the student circle first the A's, B's, then C's etc.
2. Practice circling for all letters of the alphabet.
3. Have student "track", using a small flashlight, as he or she follows the print.
4. Using a newspaper, have student circle A's in one color, connect, then B's, etc., to provide tracking practice in context.
5. Remind student to move only eyes, when scanning a page for letters or words.
6. Use a pacing device, or hold a bookmark or index card under each line.
7. (Using a patch) do each of the following with right, then left eye.

    A. Read each letter from left to right.

    B. Read each second letter from left to right.

    C. Read each third letter from left to right.

    D. Repeat using metronome or pencil tapping to set a beat.

    E. Make large cards with varying combination of letters.

    1. F R G H X E Y N K S W H I O K G G T

    2. G v n c x s d g h j k l o I u y t r t e w s s d g v e x z s

8. Have student stand and hold book or reading material in both hands. Have student start at the upper left side of the page, quickly reading the first and last letters of each line. Next, read the first and last letter of each line starting at the bottom of the page, and going up.

Wall Chart

Using the accompanying wall chart (enlarged) (and eye patch, if desired) have student "read" the eye chart, from left to right, one line at a time, one eye, then the other. Use a metronome, or tap a beat with pencil or other, to accompany. Next, read first and last letter in each line, and in any other order you desire, for visual tracking practice.

P	L	T	N	D	H	C	O
H	V	C	Z	E	L	S	N
T	U	V	P	R	U	Z	H
F	D	N	B	C	T	V	F
C	Y	R	S	P	E	O	C
E	O	T	D	L	S	N	B
B	R	P	E	Z	O	D	C
A	X	F	S	P	D	O	T

WHAT THEY NEED TO KNOW

BASIC SKILLS TO BE MASTERED AT EMERGENT & EARLY LEVELS

(K–3 Skill Levels)

Concrete Word Play: Can build simple words, including own name, using materials such as playdough or wax sticks.

Phonemic Awareness: (smallest unit of speech: the individual sounds). Recognizes rhymes, matches letters and words, hears syllables, blends sounds, knows word families.

Print Awareness: Recognizes environmental print, functional print, and dramatic play. Basic elements of print, book handling, directionality, left to right eye sweeps, etc.

Syntactic Awareness: Understands how phrases and sentences work, word order, me chanics, such as capitals, periods, and commas. The structure of the language is important to learn.

Letter Recognition: Recognizes upper and lower case letters, all letter names and shapes. Teach upper and lower case for each letter, simultaneously.

Word Families: Recognizes the basic onsets and rimes which make up over 500 words, by the end of third grade.

Decoding: Teach kids these strategies: sound out, compare to other known words (cross checking), use the three cueing systems, use picture clues, look for little word in bigger words, look at the shape of words, use the context, reread the word or sentence to self correct. Practice, practice, practice.

Writing: Ensure by the end of kindergarten, child scribbles with invented spellings, writes own name, participates in language-experience stories. By the end of first grade, uses more conventional spelling, uses some beginning grammar, writes sentences and simple stories. By the end of second and third grades, uses more advanced grammar and conventional spelling. Write continually, to reinforce reading. Logs and journals work from kindergarten on.

Vocabulary: By the end of first grade, understands new words from context. By the end of third grade, knows syllabication, structural analysis tools, including prefixes and suffixes. Practice using new words continually.

Comprehension: In kindergarten and first grade, uses photos or pictures as context clues. By the end of first grade, reads to find out meaning. In first through third grade, uses prediction and summarizing. Help children understand their reading by connecting with prior knowledge and teach them to question, predict, clarify, and summarize when they read. Use a variety of graphic organizers such as Web, Venn Diagrams, etc. Reciprocal teaching is a good comprehension builder. Two students, or the teacher and student take turns reading to each other and answering questions about what has just been read. Read ing widely is the best strategy to boost children's comprehension.

FAVORITE
K-2 LIBRARY BOOKS

1. *Mike Mulligan's Steam Shovel* (Burton)
2. *The Little House* (Burton)
3. *Tell The Time With Thomas* (Awdry, Stott)
4. *The Snowy Day* (Keats)
5. *Stone Soup* (Brown)
6. *Madeline* (Bemelmens)
7. *Five Little Monkeys Jumping on the Bed* (Christlow)
8. *Rosie's Walk* (Hutchins)
9. *Shoes* (Winthrop)
10. *Tikki Tikki Tembo* (Mosel)
11. *Strega Nona* (dePaola)
12. *Mary Wore Her Red Dress & Henry Wore His Green Sneakers* (Peek)
13. *Ira Sleeps Over* (Waber)
14. *Jesse Bear, What Will You Wear?* (Carlstrom)
15. *Love You Forever* (Munsch)
16. *Millions of Cats* (Gag)
17. *Corduroy* (Freeman)
18. *Bear Shadow* (Asch)
19. *Everybody Cooks Rice* (Dooley)
20. *If You Give A Mouse A Cookie* (Numeroff)
21. *Caps For Sale* (Slobodkina)
22. *Albert's Alphabet* (Tryon)
23. *The Doorbell Rang* (Hutchins)
24. *Make Way For Ducklings* (McCloskey)
25. *Yo Yes* (Raschka)
26. *Aunt Flossie's Hats (And Crab Cakes Later)* (Howard)
27. *Cinderella Penguin or The Little Glass Flipper* (Perlman)
28. *A Bicycle For Rosaura* (Barbot)
29. *The Little Island* (MacDonald & Weisgard)
30. *Froggie Gets Dressed* (London)
31. *Mortimer Mooner Makes Lunch* (Edwards)
32. *Let's Read Together, This Old Man* (Ladybird)
33. *Silly Willy* (Cocca-Leffler)
34. *A Helpful Alphabet of Friendly Objects* (Updike)
35. *There's An Ant In Anthony* (Most)
36. *Rain* (Kalan)
37. *The Carrot Seed* (Krauss)
38. *Action Alphabet* (Rotner)
39. *Chrysanthemum* (Henkes)
40. *What's Your Name? From Ariel to Zoe* (Sanders)
41. *Leo The Late Bloomer* (Kraus)

... of course, Dr. Seuss Books

LIBRARY BOOK DECODING SAMPLER

(Skill Levels K–2)

ALPHABET

- *A Helpful Alphabet of Friendly Objects*—photos of objects, predictable patterns.

- *Action Alphabet*—movement, moving through the alphabet.

- *Albert's Alphabet*—prediction, mostly pictures, sight words.

- *What's Your Name, From Ariel to Zoe*—photos, multi-ethnic, fabulous possibilities.

FIRST BOOKS

- *Yo Yes*—sight words, predictable patterns, punctuation.

- *There's An Ant In Anthony*—predictable patterns, phonemic awareness, <u>ain</u> word family.

- *Silly Willy*—rebus, sight words, rhythms, predictable patterns.

- *Rain*—configuration, color words, <u>ain</u> word family, blends, sequence.

- *Let's Read Together, This Old Man*—rhyming, predictable patterns, sight words.

   The Carrot Seed—predictable patterns, sequence, sight words.

LANGUAGE EXPERIENCE

- *Shoes*

- *Aunt Flossie's Hat (And Crab Cakes Later)*—blends and <u>at</u> word family.

PHONICS & PREDICTABLE PATTERNS

- *Mike Mulligan's Steam Shovel*—repetition, rhythm, predictable patterns, consonant 'm', blends, hard & soft 'c', compound words.

- *Bear Shadow*—repetition, rhythm, predictable patterns, <u>sh</u> digraph, contractions, sequence.

- *Make Way For Ducklings*—digraphs, blends, contractions, predictable patterns, rhythm, <u>ack</u> word family.

- *A Bicycle For Rosaura*—rhythm, predictable patterns, prediction, compound words.

- *I Love You Forever*—rhythm, predictable patterns, sight words, sequence, compound words, contractions.

- *Cinderella Penguin*—substitution (Flipper for Slipper), quotation marks ("ears"), blends, digraphs, compound words, prefixes.
- *Froggie Gets Dressed*—word play, blends, repetition, predictable patterns, rhythm.
- *The Little House*—sight words, predictable patterns, seasons, double consonants, compound words, sequence, same and different.
- *Tell Time With Thomas*—time, compound words, sight words, blends, 'r' controlled vowels, magic 'e'.
- *Caps For Sale*—prediction, <u>ap</u> word family, color words, sequence, predictable patterns, directionality.
- *Shoes*—<u>ight</u> word family, rhyming, double consonants, digraphs, 'r' controlled vowels, magic 'e', sight words, predictable patterns, <u>ing</u> endings, seasons.
- *Snowy Day*—antonyms (happy/sad), consonant digraphs and blends, repetition, contractions, rhythm, directionality, sight words, compound words, seasons, feelings.
- *Madeline*—sequencing, blends, rhythm/rhyme, antonyms, sight words, plurals, compound words, contractions, predictable patterns, <u>ight</u> word family.
- *Mary Wore Her Red Dress*—predictable patterns, rhythm, <u>ink</u> and <u>ight</u> word families, sight words, short and long vowels.

- *Tikki Tikki Tembo*—contractions, digraphs, predicable patterns, rhythm.
- *Stone Soup*—contractions, compound words, soft 'c' sound, prefixes, prediction, sequence, etc.
- *Strega Nona Meets Her Match*—syllables, compound words, contractions, etc.
- *Everybody Cooks Rice*—compound words, <u>ice</u> word family, magic 'e'.
- *Chrysanthemum*—four syllable words, prediction, names and feelings, sequence.
- *Corduroy*—rhythm, predictable patterns, contractions, hard 'c', sight words.
- *If You Give A Mouse A Cookie*—predictable patterns, cause & effect, sequencing.
- *Ira Sleeps Over*—repetition, rhythm, predictable patterns, sequence, prediction.

COUNTING BOOKS

- *Mortimer Mooner Makes Lunch*—rhythm, predictable pattern, counting, sequencing.
- *Millions of Cats*—hard 'c', number sense, prediction, repetition, rhythm, <u>at</u> word family.
- *The Doorbell Rang*—counting, sharing theme, fractions, sight words, predictable pattern, contractions, sequencing.

COUNTING BOOKS

- *Mortimer Mooner Makes Lunch*—rhythm, predictable pattern, counting, sequencing.

- *Millions of Cats*—hard 'c', number sense, prediction, repetition, rhythm, <u>at</u> word family.

- *The Doorbell Rang*—counting, sharing theme, fractions, sight words, predictable pattern, contractions, sequencing.

  Five Little Monkeys Jumping On The Bed—sequencing, counting, rhythm, predictable patterns, chantable rhyme.

SEQUENCING FAVORITES

- *The Little Island*—sequencing, seasons, rhythm, rhyme, predictable pattern.

DIRECTIONALITY / PREPOSITIONS

- *Rosie's Walk*—sight words, spatial concepts.

Other Favorites

TEACH BASIC PHONICS

(SKILL LEVELS 1–3, OR GAPS)

TEACH

There are two goals of instruction. First, help your students recognize sound/symbol correspondences. Second, give sufficient practice in figuring out the patterns in new words.

PRACTICE

1. Teach direct instruction or short mini-lessons which are in five to twenty minute increments.

2. Teach phonics in context, using multi-modal techniques.

3. Teach only the high utility generalizations, not the exceptions. Point out Schwa sound. (unsound, as elephant).

4. Teach high frequency sight words. Especially *concrete* words.

5. When you teach each sound, have students clap it out. (long—say names) Say "a" (clap), "e" (clap), "i" (clap), "o" (clap), and "u" (clap). Then repeat the patterns, doing the short sounds

6. Point and say: (Short) "a" as in *lap*, (or *back*), "e" as in *leg*, "i" as in *lip*, "o" as in *on* (or *knock*), "u" as in *up*, (or *under*); (Long) "a" as in *table*, "e" as in *see* (or *me*), "i" as in I, "o" as in *open*, "u" as in *Universe*, (or other "u" word).

7. Make up a vowel or consonant song to a familiar tune, such as: *Row Row Row Your Boat, If You're Happy And You Know It, Happy Birthday, I'm A Little Teapot, Farmer In The Dell, Itsy Bitsy Spider,*

   London Bridge, Mary Had A Little Lamb, This Old Man, Twinkle Twinkle Little Star, etc.

8. **Three Cueing Systems**

   A. *Semantics*—the meaning, "Does this make sense? Look at the picture again. Reread the sentence."

   B. **Syntactics** —the structure, "Does this sound right to you? Can you say this another way? What other word might fit here?"

   C *Graphophonics*—print and sound symbol correspondence. "Does this look right to you? What sound or letter does it begin with? Point to the letter (word)."

   Also Say:

   "Does this look familiar? Take another look at this. What does this letter (word) look like? Point at the letter (word). Look for the little word within the big word. Check (cross reference) this word with one you know."

9. Use mini-centers, reading manipulatives, loads of reading and practice. Budding readers need *rhyme, rhythm, repetition* and *predictable patterns.* Research says that to learn a new word, students need four-fifteen exposures. Do lots of *Modeling* and *Immersion.*

10. Use quality literature, including a mix of old favorites, and new books. Use books that reinforce specific skills, especially with predictable patterns.

11. Lesson format suggestions:

    • Provide a strong, introductory SET.

    • Review yesterday's sound, letter, word, pattern etc.

    • Introduce today's (new) sound, letter, word, concept, or pattern.

    • Read a new story or article which reinforces the new concept.

    • Find the concept in print, books, or 'reading the room'.

    • Do a strong CLOSE.

    • Reinforce with practice & repetition.

PHONICS CHANTS

Have fun with these chants. Oral chants work really well, at all levels. Kids love this!

Vowels

A (clap); E (clap); I (clap); O (clap); U (clap).

Magic "E"

"E on the end makes the first vowel long." (Say in sing song voice).

Consonants

A *Digraph* has two letters, one sound. (Hold up two fingers, then one finger.) A *Blend* has two letters, and two sounds. (Hold up two fingers, then two fingers again). Then do three letter blends—hold up three fingers, then three fingers again. Chant "two letter blends have two sounds (clap, clap). Three letter blends have three sounds" (clap, clap, clap).

Compound Words

"You take two words, then squash them together." Stretch arms out, then pull back together, as you say the chant.

Contractions

"You take the letter out, then put the apostrophe in." (Do visually, with your finger) (I am = I'm)

Prefixes/Suffixes

"Prefix comes before (Lean to left); Suffix comes after (Lean to right)." Repeat frequently.

Syllables

"Ninja know-it-all says hi-ya!"* (Say as your finger slices down to divide each syllable.) Model on board.

Paper Plate Spelling

"If you've got an R, come on up, E...; A...; D... What does it spell? READ!" etc. (Enclosed).

Credit: *Ninja originated from teachers sharing at a San Diego, California County Office workshop as I modeled creating shapes from potholder loops. I refined this to 'know-it-all' status, which kids love.

PHONICS SONGS SAMPLER

(Skill Levels 1–3)

Tune #1 (*Did You Ever Find A Lassie?*)
  Digraphs:
Teacher:
    Would you like to find some *digraphs,* some *digraphs,* some *digraphs?*
    Would you like to find some *digraphs?*
    Two letters with **one** sound.
Class:
We love to find some *digraphs,* some *digraphs,* some *digraphs.* We love to find some
  digraphs, **two** letters with **one** sound.
    Like *th* and *sh* and *ch* and *ph*
    We love to find some *digraphs*
    Two letters with **one** sound.

Tune #2 (*If You're Happy and You Know It*)
  Blends:
If it's a *blend* and you know it, clap your hands (clap, clap).
If it's a *blend* and you know it, clap your hands (clap, clap).
If it's a *blend* and you know it, your smile will certainly show it.
If it's a *blend* and you know it, clap your hands, (clap, clap).

When a *blend* has **two** letters there's **two** sounds (clap, clap). When a *blend* has **three**
letters, there's **three** sounds (clap, clap, clap).

If it's a *blend* and you know it, your *smile* will certainly show it.
If it's a *blend* and you know it, clap your hands (clap, clap).

A **two** letter blend has **two** sounds (clap, clap).
A **three** letter blend has **three** sounds (clap, clap, clap).

If it's a blend and you know it, your smile will certainly show it.
If it's a blend and you know it, clap your hands (clap, clap).

Tune #3 *(I'm a Little Teapot)*
I'm a little magic 'e'
Here's what I can do
When I'm on the end of a word, the first vowel is long

If I am away that day
There's nothing I can do
The first vowel sound stays short
Here are just a few
bath and bathe, and pin and pine, cut and cute, and shin and shine

I'm a little magic 'e'
There's so much that I do.

Songs are fun to sing, fun to write, and fun to create with kids of all ages. Record! This is a wonderful tool to stimulate memory. Use it as much as possible. You write and perform, to model, then have your students write (and perform). Do songs at any level. It works!

YOUR TURN:
- **Concept to teach:**

- **Original Tune:**

- **Your Song:**

TEACH OR REVIEW
EASY START DECODING SEQUENCE
SHORTCUT: BASIC WORD RECOGNITION SKILLS

TEACH

1. *Phonemic Awareness*
   (word play)

2. *The Alphabet*
   (letter games)

3. *Phonics Fundamentals*
   A. CONSONANTS
   (special emphasis on c, g, q, s, y, w)
   Digraphs: Ch, Sh, Th, Wh, Ph, Gh, Ck, Ng
   (Initial, Medial, Final)
   Blends: (2 letter) Bl, Br, Cl, Cr, Dr, Fl, Fr,
   Gl, Gr, Pl, Pr, Sc, Sk, Sl, Sm, Sn, Sp, St,
   Sw, Fr, Tw; (3 letter) Scr, Spr, Str, Spl, Squ, Thr
   B. VOWELS: A, E, I, O, U
   (Short, Long): a, e, i, o, u

   (See teaching tips)

Vowel Teams: ae, ai, ee, ea, ie, oa, ei, ue, ui

Magic 'e': ate, ite, etc.

'R' Controlled (Bossy R): ar, er, ir, or, ur

Diphthongs: au, aw, ew, ey, oi, ou, ow, oo, oy

4. *Word Families*

5. *Structural Analysis*
   Compound Words

   Prefixes and Suffixes
   Syllables
   Contractions
   (Accent)

6. *Sight Words* (Vocabulary)

7. *Cueing System*
   Graphophonic ("Does it look right?")
   Syntactic ("Does it sound right?")*
   Semantic ("Does it make sense?")

*Note Syntactic doesn't work well for second language learners. Use another cue.

---

*Teach skills in Mini-Lessons or during
"teachable" moments. Practice daily, as often as possible.
See accompanying decoding practice pages.*

Note: Never teach exceptions. When they come up say "that's an exception."

SUCCESS SECRET

PLAY WITH PHONEMIC AWARENESS

(Skill Levels: K–3 , ELL or gaps)

TEACH
- Rhythm & Rhyme
- Parts of Word (Synthesis; Segmenting)
- Sequence of Sounds (beginning, middle, end)
- Substitution of Sounds

- Blending

PRACTICE
- Phonemic Awareness—Word Play, Teaching Sounds and Letters That Match
1. **Things to say** *to students:*
- What sound does your name start with?
- What's another word that begins with this sound?
- What's the first sound in this word? Nod your head, clap your hands, wiggle your hips, etc. when you hear the first sound in the word. st sound in the word. st sound in the word.

RHYMING BOXES

1	2
3	4

3. **Tell me a word round**—*that rhymes with...*

4. **Listening for sounds**
- Use a tissue to feel vibrations. Put a tissue in front of your mouth, as you model. See which sounds move the tissue most. Put your fingers on your throat and feel different sounds.

5. **Yes—No Cards**
- When kids hear two rhyming words, hold up yes, if they don't rhyme, *no*. (Scratch paper or index cards)

6. **Alliteration Games**
- Silly Susie sells seashells. Busy bumblebees bumped into the bear. Billy Buttons built boxes. (Teacher shared.)

7. **Rhyming Songs**
- *Ba Bay* (substitution).

8. **Make substitutions**
- Lots of word play. Slipper—flipper—zipper, etc.

9. **Rhyming fun**
- What rhymes with *house*?
- What doesn't rhyme... cat, mat, rat, dump, etc.

10. **Which words begin**—*with the same sound? (Peas, pickles, nuts, pears, etc.)*

11. **Putting sounds together**—blending: s-u-n—sun. (Do out loud)

12. **Props: sounds & rhyming**
- What word would these sounds make? C-a-t; cat.

13. **Substitutions**
- Draw three boxes on the board. Keep substituting the initial consonant

(B)(C)(P)	A	T

14. **Copy cat**—sound like me! (Make sounds, students follow.)

15. **Name Chant**
A. It begins with T ends with im (or next comes)—Tim.
B. Begins with T, ends with im—put them together and it spells Tim. Do other names.

16. **Where's The Sound?** Show me!

head	waist	feet
beginning	middle	end

17. **Tap your foot**—when you hear the LAST sound in the word.

- Touch your waist when you hear the sound in the middle.
- Tap your chopstick, (pencil) on the desk when you hear the same sound... (different sound).
- (While showing.) Find the letter that makes this sound like (blank) in your book.
- Find this letter written somewhere in the room. (Look around room.)
- Point to the letter that makes this sound. (Around room, in book.)

18. **Which sound first?**

- Book (or another word). What sound did you hear first?

19. **Rhyming books**

- Use books with rhyme, repetition, and predictable patterns. (Resource guide.)

20. **Rhyming Round**

- I baked my cake, then swam in the lake. Ooey, gooey egg, is dripping down my leg. etc.*

21. **Clap clap snap snap**—sounds, letters.

22. **Clap your hands** if the word starts (ends) with a _____

23. **Rhythm/category** round game.

24. **Heads & tails**

- Hear the sound at the head (beginning) or end (tail). Draw it (Like a dog or cat).

25. *Sound fluency*

- Pick one sound at a time. Kids say as many words as possible, making that sound, within one minute increments.

26. **Last letter round**

- I'm thinking of a word: eat; toe; elephant; time; easy, etc. (Use last letters)... Or first letter round).

27. **How many sounds** do you hear?

C	A	T		

How many letters? (Show me–three).

Use fingers to show

Or

How many sounds?

Tree has three sounds, four letters.

28. **Sorts**

- Start by sorting pictures or words by initial sounds, final consonants, short or long vowels, initial consonants, (blends, digraphs), etc.

29. **"Sounds in the word** are C-A-T and that makes the word cat." Etc.

30. **Pop Up Words**

- Three kids, beginning, middle, end. "Pop up when I say your letter" (sound).

* Anonymous teacher favorite

TIPS!

a. Use a feather—write the word in the air using the feather, or trace each letter on the feather. *Or* blow sounds onto the feather.

b. Take a clean toothbrush- tracing on students' backs is better than just using your finger.

c. Find the letter around the room. When you "read the room", walls, etc. students may use a pointer, chopstick, clean fly swatter, etc.

d. A beach ball is fun to bat around, saying the letter. Write big letters on the ball, with permanent magic marker (Multi-sensory).

e. Use mirrors- kids watch their mouths and throats as they make sounds.

f. Use a 'phonics phone' (plumber's elbow) to clearly hear the sound. Speak into the phone.

g. Use 'Framers' as you 'read the room' and find letters in books, newspapers, and magazines. (Twist pipe cleaner into a loop.)

h. Chanting, singing help reinforce the word play.

i. REPEAT! REPEAT! REPEAT!

j. Practice as often as possible, daily.

AWESOME ALPHABET IDEAS

(Skill Levels: K—1, ELL or gaps)

Start with easiest sounds first. Start with sounds kids can feel vibrating in their throats, such as *m.* Teach *a letter a day*, then repeat like crazy. Begin with easy consonants, adding in basic vowels. Teach upper and lower case letters together.

Fast Fun Activities To Reinforce Letters:

1. Alphabet trade books! (Lots.)
2. Names and name games.
3. Alphabet Bingo.
4. Sing the alphabet song.
5. Word Walls.
6. Letter books, made by kids.
7. Tactile letters of all sorts: blocks, sponges, magnetic letters, cubes, stampers, etc.
8. Wax stick letters.
9. Modeling compound letters.
10. Label letters on bean bags with permanent magic marker.
11. Alliteration book.
12. Alphabet picture matching.
13. Environmental print.
14. Letter 'round' games.
15. Alphabet flash cards.
16. Alphabet music.
17. Act it Out Alphabet: B—bouncing; C—catching; W—walking, etc.
18. Parts of Body Alphabet; A—arm; E—elbow; etc.
19. Jump rope to Alphabet, chanting the letters.
20. Write the alphabet.
21. Body letters—form the letters—upper and lower case (standing, sitting, lying on the floor, alone or with partners).
22. Letter Bag—Write the letter on the outside; inside, load with small props.
23. Alphabet Pop-Ups, mini books, or flip books (student made).
24. Teacher Apron—felt apron; attach felt letters; or Velcro apron—attach Velcro letters or tiny props.
25. Make up little songs about the letters.
26. Use rhythm instruments to accompany chanting, singing the alphabet.
27. Give each child a chopstick to point to letters when you "Read the Room" (the print).
28. Write letters in the air or on varied tactile surfaces.
29. Make letter jackets out of butcher paper, cuting arm holes. Write a giant letter on each, using tempera paint or permanent magic marker. Move students around to form words.
30. Make finger paint bags to trace letters and words... Using a snack size baggie, fill with 2-3 tablespoons of a bright primary colored finger paint. Seal well and check for leaks. Students trace letters, (words) on top with finger or a q-tip. (No mess, fun, effective.)

CONSONANTS

TEACH

What is a consonant sound? All letters, other than vowels. Model. Use props from home for more sensory activities.

PRACTICE

1. Teach single consonant sounds, first. Teach easy to do sounds.

2. Match consonants with key words (b as in bed). Model on board, and orally.

3. Match consonant sounds with words listed or read orally.

4. 'Read the room' (wall print) matching sounds with letters, as you go.

5. List as many words as possible for each sound.

6. Find consonants in classroom books. Provide for tracing and writing time.

7. Start basic word bank or folder. (Easy Start Word Bank,)

8. Do the Word Wall. Separate consonants from vowels.

9. Teach single letter consonants, then consonant blends and digraphs (either order).

10. Practice. Repeat. Repeat. Repeat. Do mini-lessons.

11. Teach a letter a day. (A letter a week is too slow.) Review constantly.

EASY START BLENDS, DIGRAPHS

Blends

bl	br	sk	squ
cl	cr	sm	str
fl	dr	sn	thr
gl	fr	sp	tw
p1	gr	st	st
sl	pr	sw	nt
spl	tr	scr	sn
dw	sc	spr	nd

Digraphs

wh	ph
ch	gh
th	ck
sh	ng

> ### Sample Word Games
> 1. Say as many blend (digraph) words as you can in a minute.
> 2. Write as many blend (digraph) words as you can in a minute.
> 3. With the whole class, group, or pairs, say as many of each type, alternating word types.

CONSONANT DIGRAPHS

TEACH

Digraphs are two consonants standing together which make up one sound. Consonant digraphs are: wh, ch, th, sh, ph, gh, ck, ng. They can be at the beginning, middle, or end of a word.

DRILL ACTIVITY

(Say out loud, as a chant, with the whole class, small group, or individual.)

Digraphs	
Wh	*When* and…
Ch	*Chew, nachos, French* and…
Th	*Think, with* and…
Sh	*Shirt, hush* and…
Ph	*Phone, photo* and…
Gh	*Laugh, cough* and…
Ck	*Clock* and…
Ng	*Spelling* and…

PRACTICE

1. Show objects ('concretes'), photos or overheads of things that start with consonant digraphs.

2. Students say or write the digraph for each object shown by teacher.

3. Give a list of words on board or paper. Have the class underline, circle, or place a triangle around the digraphs.

4. Do the Digraph Chant: "A digraph has two letters" (hold up two fingers), "and one sound" (hold up one finger).

5. Find digraphs on a newspaper page. Mark them. Share as a class; add to your lists.

6. Find digraphs in classroom books. (Use fun framers to frame digraphs.)

7. List digraph words on classroom Word Wall. (Frame them.)

8. Students write in word banks or word folder.

9. Make digraph flip books or pop-up cards.

10. Kids can play Digraph Bingo, or other games. Make up songs, cheers, jump rope, jingles and chants about digraphs.

11. Drill orally as often as possible daily.

DIGRAPH BINGO
(FOUR BOX FOLD)

1.	2.
3.	4.

1. Make a four box fold or use the accompanying page.
2. Call out a word; students place marker on the digraph.
3. Call out a digraph; students write words having that digraph.

FOUR BOX FOLD REPRODUCIBLE

1	2
3	4

CONSONANT BLENDS

TEACH

Tell students: A consonant blend is a combination of two or more consonants together (in one syllable). Each letter holds (says) its own sound.

PRACTICE

1. Chant: "A two letter blend has two letters (hold up two fingers) and two sounds". "A three letter blend has three letters and three sounds" (hold up three fingers).

2. Put a list of words on the board, or on paper. Have students underline, circle, or put a triangle around the blends.

3. Give a list of just the blends. (List enclosed.) Students have set time period to write as many blend words as possible. (Three minutes approximately.) Time it.

4. "Read the Room" (wall print) pointing to words with blends.

5. Find blends in classroom books.

6. Name objects in the room that begin with blends.

7. Make up sentences with blend words.

8. Make a list of as many words as possible from each blend.

9. Play Blend Bingo, chant, or sing songs.

10. For a fun visual for younger students draw a kitchen blender on the board and putting blends together, blend in the blender, using a blending movement.

11. Use the time-tested teacher trick, 'slap the blends'. Use a flyswatter with a triangle or square cut out of it to frame blends on wall print.

12. Find as many blends as possible on a newspaper page or other print and mark them.

13. Write a sentence or paragraph using as many blend words as possible.

14. Practice blends as often as possible, daily.

BLEND BINGO

1. Use this blends, or select eight at a time from the Easy Start List, and use the accompanying eight box fold.

2. Call out a word. Students find the blend in that word

3. Reverse; call out the blend. Students have to write words having that blend.

gl	fr	st	pr
scr	str	fn	pl
cr	sc	sm	sl
dr	br	bl	sp
sw	fl	spr	cl
sp	tw	sk	gr

EIGHT BOX FOLD REPRODUCIBLE

1	2
3	4
5	6
7	8

SILENT LETTER RULES

TIP: Teach these when you teach the constonants

1. When "c" is together with kin a one syllable word, the "c" is silent. (Clock)
2. When "gh" comes at the end or near the end of a word, it's silent. (Though)
3. When "gh" is with "t" the "gh" is silent. (Light)
4. When "k" comes before "n" in a word, the "k" is silent. (Knee)
5. When "w" comes before "r" in a word the "w" is silent. (Write)
6. When "t" comes in the middle of a one syllable word, the "t" is silent. (Catch)

WORDS
Rule 1:
Rule 2:
Rule 3:
Rule 4:
Rule 5:
Rule 6:

Use as a wall chart, smart board, or other.
Whole class or partners

PRACTICE

C & G sounds
Coat, City, Goat, Giraffe
These activities are guaranteed to keep you guessing with genuine gusto!

1. Open your textbook to any page. Count how many words start with hard c, soft c hard g, soft g. Write at least one of the words for each hard "c" (like coat):

    _____
    _____
    _____

    Soft "c" (like city):

    _____
    _____

    Hard "g" (like goat):

    _____
    _____
    _____

    Soft "g" (like giraffe):

    _____
    _____

2. List as many hard and soft "c" and. "g" words as you can in one minute:

    _____
    _____
    _____
    _____
    _____

3. Write a paragraph using as many "c" and "g" words as you can:

    _____
    _____
    _____
    _____
    _____
    _____
    _____
    _____
    _____
    _____
    _____

4. List names starting with hard and soft c's and g's: (George, Candy, Cindy, Gertrude, etc.)

    _____
    _____
    _____
    _____
    _____
    _____

PRACTICE
Q & U GO TOGETHERS

1. Turn these words into a "Qu" Go togethers. Substitute the beginning with qu.
   * (Out loud or on paper)

Stick, Sick_____

Tack, Stack_____

Sit, Pit_____

Take, Bake_____

Teen, Seen_____

Bench, Wrench_____

Best, Test_____

Shake, Bake_____

Whiz, Fizz_____

Drill, Fill_____

Sliver, Liver_____

Pail, Rail_____

Wrote, Tote_____

Sell, Fell_____

2. Find two "Qu" words in the dictionary or glossary as quickly as you can. Learn their definitions, how to spell them, and use them often.

   Answers to part one:
   Quick
   Quack
   Quit
   Quake
   Queen
   Quench
   Quest
   Quake
   Quiz
   Quill
   Quiver
   Quail
   Quote
   Quell

3. Find as many "Qu" words as possible in a given book:

   _____
   _____
   _____
   _____
   _____
   _____
   _____
   _____
   _____

PRACTICE
'Y' AS CONSONANT, 'Y' AS VOWEL

List as many consonant 'y' words as you can think of in three minutes. Next, list words where 'y' sounds like the long 'i' vowel, then like long 'e' sound.

Like Consonant 'y'	'y' Like Long 'i'	y' Like long 'e'
Yes	**Cry**	**City**

VOWELS

TEACH

1. Introduce the vowels-a, e, i, o, u (y) (w)
2. Give key words that match vowels, such as:

Long	Short
A-apron	A-apple
E-eat	E-egg
I-ice	I-sit
O-open	O-on
U-use	U-up

Tip: f has the sound of e in pony, and the long sound of i in my. W acts as a vowel, in combination.

PRACTICE:

1. Make a chart on the board, headed long and short vowels. Have the students correctly mark which column (long or short). Example:

Long	Short
Eat	Leg
Bite	Bit

2. Practice the Long Vowel Rules, out loud, or as a chant.

A. Single vowel at the end of a word is usually long (me).

B. When a one syllable word has two vowels, one of which is final 'e', the first vowel is long, final 'e' is silent (make).

C. When two vowels are together in a word, the first is long, second is silent (meet).

3. Call out, list as many short/long vowel words as possible.

4. Play games, do word rounds.

5. Write long and short vowel words in word banks or word folders students are keeping.

6. "Read the Room", pointing out long and short vowel words.

7. Point out long and short vowel words in books and online..

8. Play vowel bingo, make up poems about vowels, do chants, raps and cheers.

9. Practice writing vowels and words with vowels.

10. Pass a Koosh ball or other, around class, saying a short or long vowel word.

11. Play jump rope, saying vowel jingles.

12. PRACTICE.

PRACTICE
SHORT VOWEL GAME

Fill in the blanks and create as many new words as possible. Do these, then more, on your own, with a partner, or in a small group.

b	**-**	**d**

(bad,bed,bid,bud)

b	**-**	**g**

(bag, beg, big, bog, bug)

f	**-**	**n**

(fan, fin, fun)

s	**-**	**t**

(sat, set, sit)

TEACH THE MAGIC 'E' RULE

TEACH

Magic 'E' is fun to work with; this rule is about 75% utility, definitely worth teaching. Chant "E on the end makes the first vowel long." Write three examples such as: cut-cute; hid-hide; bath-bathe. (Other 'E' words are: pin-pine; shin-shine; mop-mope; plan-plane, etc). Act out each word to ensure understanding.

PRACTICE

2 Ways To Teach 'E' Rule:

Method 1

hid	e

Take an index card (3 x 5 or 4 x 6). Draw a line and fold. Fold over on right or fold right side of card over, approximately 1". Write a large small case 'e' on the right. (If you flip the card over you'd see only an e', nothing else). Write a word such as Tim on left. Fold the hidden e over; say, "Tim becomes Time," etc. Model several, then the students make some sample models for practice.

Method 2

Create a fold. Use graph paper, or create a grid with four or five boxes across; the number of boxes shown is determined by the number of 'E' words you are using to reinforce the skill, and number of letters per word. Model, then students cut across, under the e's, all the way down the page; fold all the e's back. Then one at a time, unfold

P	I	N	E
C	U	T	E
K	I	T	E

each 'e' on each line, as bath becomes bathe, etc.

Act out each concept, one word at a time, as "I have on a pin. Pin becomes pine, like a pine tree."

Be sure to follow up by finding Magic 'E' words in print—books, etc. See accompanying Easy Start Magic 'E' list, and reproducible of the 'E' fold.

OTHER MAGIC 'E' IDEAS:

MAGIC 'E' REPRODUCIBLE

p	i	n	<u>e</u>
m	a	n	<u>e</u>
c	u	b	<u>e</u>
f	a	d	<u>e</u>
h	i	d	<u>e</u>
c	a	n	<u>e</u>
m	o	p	<u>e</u>
r	i	p	<u>e</u>
c	a	p	<u>e</u>

p	i	n	<u>e</u>
m	a	n	<u>e</u>
c	u	b	<u>e</u>
f	a	d	<u>e</u>
h	i	d	<u>e</u>
c	a	n	<u>e</u>
m	o	p	<u>e</u>
r	i	p	<u>e</u>
c	a	p	<u>e</u>

EASY START MAGIC 'E' LIST

Magic 'E'

'E' at the end rule: E on the end makes the first vowel long.

pin	pine	fad	fade
hat	hate	plan	plane
pal	pale	kit	kite
shin	shine	cap	cape
pet	Pete	hid	hide
car	care	cut	cute
win	whine	bath	bathe
mad	made	rat	rate
Tim	time	mat	mate
fin	fine	fat	fate
mop	mope	nap	nape
tin	tine	rip	ripe
star	stare	strip	stripe
man	mane	pip	pipe
cub	cube	lop	lope
par	pare	can	cane
war	ware	pan	pane
tap	tape	scrap	scrape
grip	gripe	glob	globe

OTHER WORDS AND IDEAS:

'R' CONTROLLED VOWELS (BOSSY 'R')*

TEACH
Chant together.

Vowel+R	Key Word
A + R=AR	CAR
E + R=ER	HER
I + R=IR	GIRL
O + R=OR	FOR
U + R=UR	HURT

PRACTICE

1. Have students "Read the Room", pointing to 'r' controlled vowels.
2. Give students a list of words. Circle the words which have 'r' controlled vowels.
3. Underline 'r' controlled vowels on a newspaper page. or other print.
4. List as many 'r' controlled words as possible in a designated time period (three minutes approximate or more).
5. Bossy 'R' fold activity (enclosed).
6. Students write bossy 'r' words in their word banks.
7. List on classroom Word Wall.
8. Write a sentence or paragraph using as many bossy 'r' words as possible.
9. Make sets of flash cards and word rings for students to practice with each other.
10. Take home a set of flash cards and word rings, for practice.
11. Make a bossy 'r' pop up card. Practice as often as possible, daily.

*"R" controlled vowels, Bossy 'R', and vowel plus R are all the same.

PRACTICE
TWO BOX FOLD BOSSY 'R'
'R' CONTROLLED VOWELS

Bossy 'R'	Words
ar	far, car, star
er	her
ir	stir, first
or	sailor, tutor
ur	tum, blur, hurt
1. ar	
2. er	
3. ir	
4. or	
5. ur	

1. Fold paper into two columns (hot dog fold).
2. Model Bossy 'R'. List words for each category.
3. On the right side of the fold, students list as many 'r' controlled words as possible.

VOWEL DIPHTHONGS & VOWEL DIGRAPHS

TEACH

A. VOWEL DIPHTHONGS

These are sometimes called whiners or screamers, as they make an unusual sound. When two vowels are next to each other, they make a new sound like how someone sounds when hurt, or the wind blowing. (Exaggerate when modeling.)

The most useful diphthongs to know include: <u>ow, oy, oi, ou, oo.</u> <u>Au, aw</u> are sad sounds. <u>Ew, oo, ou</u> are stinky sounds. <u>Oi</u> and <u>oy</u> are piggy sounds. <u>Ou</u> and <u>ow</u> are ouchy (pinchy) sounds.

EASY START DIPHTHONG LIST

down	boil	count	smooth
cowboy	join	found	roof
plow	soil	aloud	foil
how	toy	out	shout
now	boy	our	pout
tool	enjoy	town	

B. VOWEL DIGRAPHS (VOWEL TEAMS)

TEACH THE RULE

Two vowels that make up one speech sound are called vowel digraphs: example: <u>ee, ea, ae, oa, ai, ay, ue.</u> These are also called vowel teams. (Teach with team work example.)

meat	bead	boat	rain	say
seed	tail	float	pain	seat
braid	mean	maid	plain	weed
coat	lead	goat	near	main

PRACTICE
LONG VOWEL TEAM (DIGRAPHS)

Add another vowel right after the short vowel-it's a long sound, a vowel team and a brand new word!

1. brad_____

2. men_____

3. pant_____

4. mad_____

5. plan_____

6. red_____

7. met_____

8. man_____

9. wed_____

10. bled_____

11. cot_____

12. led_____

13. net_____

14. got_____

15. bed_____

16. set_____

17. pan_____

Vowel Digraphs:
<u>ee, ea, ae, oa, ai, ay, ue</u>

1. braid
2. mean
3. paint
4. maid
5. plain
6. read
7. meet
8. main
9. weed
10. bleed
11. coat
12. lead
13. neat
14. goat
15. bead
16. seat
17. pain

HERE'S MORE:

WORD FAMILY PATTERNS

TEACH

37 Word Families make over 500 words in English. The accompanying list has some of the more common families. You may also see families called phonograms and onsets and rimes. Onset is the beginning. Rime, the ending.

PRACTICE

1.   Use concrete objects to introduce, such as a cake box for ake, a sock for ock etc. (Depending on grade level.)

2.   'Web' the families.

WEB

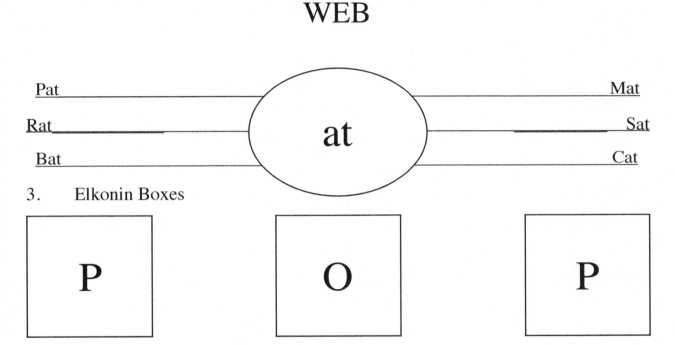

Pat —————————————— (at) —————————————— Mat

Rat ——————————————   —————————————— Sat

Bat ——————————————   —————————————— Cat

3.   Elkonin Boxes

P	O	P

4.   Manipulatives-

Magnetic tiles, paper tiles, letter cubes, lima beans. Start with one word family; have students keep substituting initial letters. Write on separate paper.

5.   Accordion Fold

See enclosed. Do paper fold. Put one family on each line of the fold-write as many words of each family on each line, as possible. (Depending on grade level.)

6.   Word Family Fan

Make accordion folds out of construction paper or tagboard, tape ends. Start with an words, keep adding. Put the fans up on a bulletin board. (Depending on grade level.)

7.   Word Family Wallet

(See enclosed.) Fill the wallet with one family per section. (Depending on grade level.)

PRACTICE
WORD FAMILY ACCORDION FOLD

1. ink:_____

2. ap::_____

3. ight::_____

4. op::_____

5. ate::_____

6. ake::_____

Fold into accordion fold pattern. (Fold on the lines.) List as many 'family' words as possible, for each family.

WALLET PATTERN REPRODUCIBLE

1.	2.	3.
(Staple)	(Staple)	(Staple)
(Fold up)	(Fold up)	(Fold up)

1. Fold 8 1/2 x 11 paper in half.
2. Fold up.
3. Fold into thirds (3 sections).
4. Staple the sections to make pockets.
5. List the word family on each line.
6. Put (scratch paper) words in pockets.
7. Practice with various word families.

EASY START WORD FAMILY LIST

ack— back, black, quack, rack, stack

ag— bag, flag, rag, sag, tag, snag, wag

ain— brain, chain, drain, main, pain, rain, train

ake— bake, brake, cake, fake, lake, make, rake, snake, take

all— ball, call, fall, hall, small, tall, wall

am— clam, ham, jam, ram, slam

ame— came, blame, fame, game, flame, lame, name, same

an— can, pan, man, fan, tan, bran

and— band, brand, grand, hand, land, sand

ap— cap, clap, flap, rap, map, snap, trap, tap

ar— far, star, par, jar, tar

at— cat, hat, flat, sat, bat, chat, mat, pat, rat

ate— date, gate, late, rate, skate, state

ay— pay, say, lay, hay, ray, may, day

ead— bread, read, lead, instead

ed— bed, fed, red, sled, led, wed

ee— bee, fee, knee, see, tree, free

eed— bleed, seed, feed, weed, need

eet— feet, meet, sheet, beet, greet

ell— bell, cell, fell, shell, spell, tell, well, yell

en— den, hen, men, then, when, pen

ent— bent, cent, vent, tent, spent, went, rent, sent, dent

et— bet, get, met, net, pet, set, wet, jet, yet

ice— dice, mice, nice, rice, slice

ig— big, pig, fig, twig, wig, dig

ight— light, right, sight, night

ill— will, bill, still, chill, fill, hill, mill

in— pin, grin, win, tin, chin, fin

ine— dine, fine, mine, vine, nine, twine, line

ing— swing, bring, string, king, ring, wing, sing

ink— ink, rink, blink, wink, sink, stink, pink, link

ip— clip, chip, dip, flip, lip, hip, ship, rip, tip

it— bit, sit, lit, fit, hit, pit, quit, wit

ite— bite, kite, white, write

oat— boat, coat, float, goat, throat

ock— block, clock, dock, lock, rock, sock

od— cod, nod, rod, pod

ode— code, rode

og— dog, frog, hog, jog, log, smog

oon— moon, noon, spoon, raccoon, soon

op— mop, stop, shop, hop, drop, crop, top

ot— hot, cot, dot, tot, pot, blot, got, rot, lot

ouse— house, mouse, douse

ub— club, cub, scrub, tub

ug— bug, hug, jug, mug, plug, tug

ump— lump, pump, dump, jump, bump

un— bun, fun, run, spun, sun

up— cup, pup

ut— cut, hut, rut, nut, shut

y— cry, fly, shy, try, why, dry, fry

PRACTICE

WORD BUILDER GAME

pr	op	st	am
ake	bl	sh	sl
ant	ame	ock	ink

1. Have students write blends, digraphs, word families, one per index card, or piece of scrap paper.

2. Placing cards or slips of paper in front of student(s) move word elements around into varying combinations. Write new words down. Use cards more than once.

3. Some possible words from this combination are prop, stop, slam, shock, shake, slant, slink, blink, block, stock, blame, stink. (Advanced—slake).

4. Close the activity by calling for various combinations of new words.

5. Do activity often, changing blends, digraphs, word families, to make many different words.

Chapter 4
Teach Structural Analysis

Great ways to teach students how the English language is structured

This chapter stresses the importance of teaching structural analysis skills including contractions, compound words, syllables, roots, prefixes and suffixes. **'Reading Champions'** comprehensive structural analysis strategies help teachers at school and at-home plan enticing lessons. It is imperative that these skills are taught efficiently, as they are important to decoding success.

"Students understand the basic features of reading. They select letter patterns and know how to translate them ... by using phonics, syllabication and word parts" (Language Arts Standards). In order to become fluent readers by third grade and achieve *automaticity* in reading, structural analysis is a key.

Teaching Colorful Compound Words
Prefix and Suffix Games
Syllable Rules and Activities
Teaching Cool Contractions

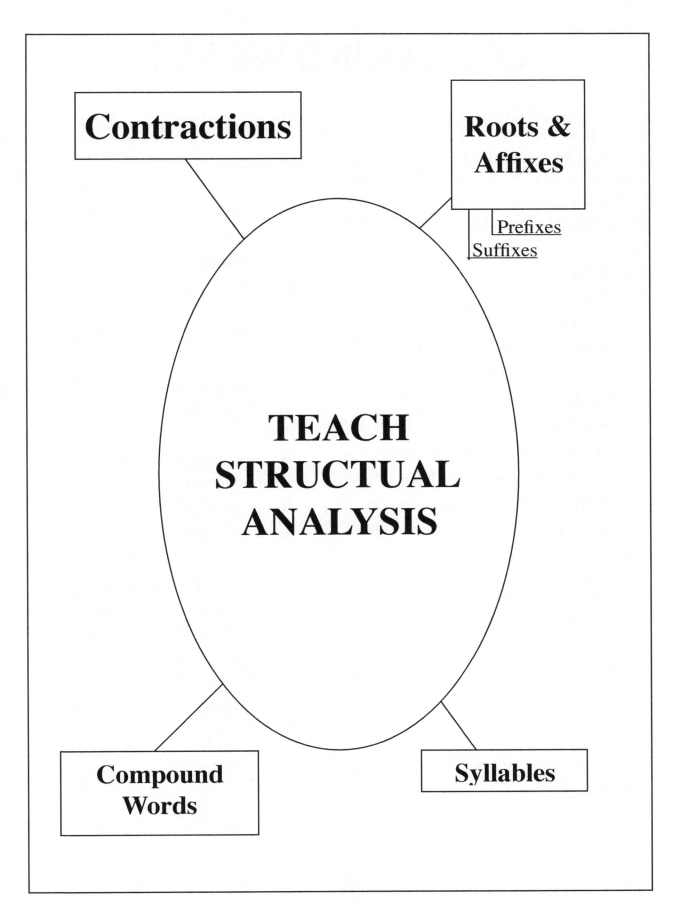

COMPOUND WORDS

TEACH

Compound words are two words standing together ('squashed' together) that make a brand new word different in meaning from the original two words.

PRACTICE

1. "Read the Room" pointing to compound words.

2. Find compound words in text-books or other print.

3. Circle compound words on a newspaper page or other print.

4. Make lists of compound words.

5. Create compound word folds.

6. Orally or on paper, make lists of compound words, then divide the words slicing between, (dog/house), or write the two words underneath (doghouse) (dog house)

7. Students put words in their word bank.

8. List on classroom Word Wall. Practice daily, or as often as possible.

9. See Compound Words practice pages.

10. Post a large compound word Anchor chart on the classroom wall.

11. Create compound words out of any modeling compound, as play dough.

12. Write sentences using as many compound words as possible.

13. When reading with the class, point out the compound words as they appear.

14. Say "Find 2 (3) compound words on page 22 (etc.). You have one minute (etc.). Begin." Write the compounds. Students add to their lists, sharing with each other.

15. Make pop-up cards or flash cards for extra practice.

TEACHING COLORFUL COMPOUND WORDS

CHANT–"You Take Two Words, and You Squash Them Together" (Use hand motions).

1. List compound words on the board. (See Easy Start Compound Word List, p.)
   Draw a line between the two words. Students write the two words that make up the compound word.

2. Look for compound words around the room.

3. Look for compound words in a textbook, library book, or other.

4. Do a 4 box fold. At the top of each box, write the word; underneath, write the two words that make up the compound word. Then draw the new word in the box.

1. lip/stick	2. cup/cake
lip stick	cup cake
3. snow/flake	4. dog/house
snow flake	dog house

5. Fold paper into a double fold.

ba se	ball

On the front put the two parts of the compound word. Turn it over and write the whole compound word.

Compound Word Match-Up

6. Hand out tagboard pieces of compound words. Let students work alone or with a partner to match up the pieces.

(front) | sail | | boat | | sailboat | (back)

7. Compound Word Folds #1—Use sentence strips, blank flash cards, plain paper or construction paper. Fold into thirds. (See enclosed sample.)

corn	field	cornfield

8. Compound Word Fold #2 (See enclosed cut & fold reproducible.)

dog	doghouse	house
cup	cupcake	cake
rain	rainbow	bow
shoe	shoelace	lace

Cut and fold Reproducible, as marked, on next page. Parts of compound words are on end, folding in to middle. Compound word is in the middle. Drawings are fun, too, on each section. Use 'concrete' compound words to work with, so students see the parts making up the new word. (For example, start with the enclosed Easy Start list. (How would you draw an 'anyone' or 'anything'?)

COMPOUND WORD FOLD

CUT & FOLD PATTERN

↓ FOLD IN

↑ FOLD IN

CUT — — — — — — — — — — CUT — — — — — —

CUT — — — — — — — — — — CUT — — — — — —

CUT — — — — — — — — — — CUT — — — — — —

COMPOUND WORD FOLDS

| 1 | Corn | Field | Cornfield |

| 2 | Tooth | Brush | Toothbrush |

| 3 | Mail | Man | Mailman |

| 4 | Basket | Ball | Basketball |

| 5 | Cup | Cale | Cupcake |

| 6 | Toe | Nail | Toenail |

| 7 | Eye | Lid | Eyelid |

| 8 | Foot | Ball | Football |

| 9 | Drum | Stick | Drumstick |

| 10 | Bee | Hive | Beehive |

| 11 | Snow | Man | Snowman |

| 12 | Tree | House | Treehouse |

| 13 | Door | Bell | Doorbell |

| 14 | Dog | House | Doghouse |

| 15 | Rain | Bow | Rainbow |

| 16 | Down | Stairs | Downstairs |

1. Use sentence strips, blank flashcards, or construction paper.
2. Fold into thirds.

PRACTICE

COLORFUL COMPOUND WORD GAME

What two words make up each new word? Points for each correct answer. (All winners!)

lipstick	cupboard	seashore
eggshell	weekend	spaceship
houseboat	bathrobe	schoolhouse
sailboat	fireworks	outdoors
sunlight	pancake	eyebrow

EASY START COMPOUND WORDS LIST

airplane	backbone	backyard	bathrobe
bathroom	basketball	baseball	bathtub
bedroom	bedtime	beehive	billfold
birdbath	broomstick	bulldog	bulldog
bullfrog	butterfly	campfire	campground
carpool	cheeseburger	classmate	classroom
coffeepot	corncob	cornfield	cowboy
cowgirl	cupboard	cupcake	daytime
dishpan	doorbell	doorway	downhill
downstairs	dragonfly	driveway	drugstore
earthquake	eggshell	eyebrow	eyelid
farmhouse	fireman	firewood	fireworks
flagpole	flashlight	flowerpot	football
footprint	footstep	gingerbread	goldfish
grandfather	grasshopper	hairbrush	handshake
handwriting	headline	homemade	homework
hopscotch	horseman	horseshoe	houseboat
houseboat	jellyfish	junkyard	lighthouse
lipstick	mailbox	mailman	moonlight
motorcycle	newspaper	northeast	northwest
notebook	outdoors	outside	paintbrush
pancake	pigtail	playground	policeman
policewoman	ponytail	popcorn	windshield
rainbow	raincoat	raindrop	rainfall
railroad	rattlesnake	rowboat	sailboat
schoolhouse	schoolroom	seashell	seashore
seaweed	sidewalk	snowball	snowflake
snowman	southeast	southwest	spaceship
springtime	starfish	steamboat	suitcase
summertime	sundown	sunlight	sunrise
sunset	sunshine	textbook	toenail
toothbrush	toothpick	turtleneck	weekend

PREFIXES & SUFFIXES

TEACH

1. Roots are the base words.
2. Prefixes are syllables added at the beginning of words that change the meaning (unhappy, redo).
3. Suffixes are endings which change the functions of the words- (sleeping, washing).
4. Chant "Prefix Comes Before; Suffix Comes After."

PRACTICE

1. "Read the Room"-wall print. Point out any prefix and suffix words.
2. Give students a word list. Give a time limit for marking first, roots, then prefixes, finally suffixes.
3. Provide a list of words. Have students make as many new words as possible, using both prefixes and suffixes.
4. Make a chart of common prefixes and suffixes. Photo copy for students' notebooks, laminate and hang on the classroom wall.

5. Play Prefix-Suffix Game.
6. Make as many words as possible from the enclosed Easy Start Lists.
7. Keep track of prefixes and suffixes that appear in textbooks and literature books.
8. Remember to say "Prefix Comes Before; Suffix Comes After," when modeling. Actually lean to the left or right, along with the kids, when you chant it, to reinforce in a multi-modal way.
9. Play word game rounds, practicing prefixes and suffixes.
10. Divide up the class into threes. Kids match prefixes and suffixes with the roots. Hold up large tagboard cards with roots, prefixes and suffixes. Do sitting at desks, holding up cards, or let students stand up and rotate around the room. Either way you prefer, have kids keep a list and add to it as new words are created.

happy	mis	ment	agree	view
re	sub	hood	treat	trust
pre	ship	er	friend	like
dis	ing	un	teach	marine
child	mail	ful	man	thought

Prefix—Suffix Game #1

1. Prepare sufficient copies for your class.

2. Cut into squares.

3. Put into snack size baggies or other.

4. Students make words using prefixes and suffixes, writing new words on separate paper.

5. Check student work.

6. Play frequently, substituting new affixes.

PREFIX-SUFFIX GAME   2

Remind students that "prefix comes before suffix."

Students make up two index cards or scratch paper. Write a large P on one card and a large S on the other.

Variation 1
Hold up a card with a word having a prefix or suffix. Students hold up either their P or S card, indicating what they know. (Choral response works!)

Variation 2
Hold up a root word. Students make as many prefix/suffix words as possible. List them on the board. Have students hold up either their P or S card for each word on the list.

PREFIX-SUFFIX GAMES

1. Make flashcards of common roots, prefixes, and suffixes. Use these to make as many new words as possible. Practice in pairs, small groups, or whole class. Chart it.

2. Select certain roots to work with. Write on the board (do at least one a day). Make as many new words as possible.

3. See which student can come up with the most prefixes, suffixes by skimming a newspaper page or other print.

4. Play Match-Up. Students select a prefix, suffix, or root from classroom Anchor wall chart and write it on an index card or scratch paper. At signal, whole class holds up responses. Make as many new words as possible, matching the others' cards. List.

5. Means The Same Game. Find words where prefixes mean the same thing as im (not), un (not), and ir (not).

   Variation 1: Add a suffix to make words meaning "full of", for example, ful (faithful), etc.

   Variation 2: Add a suffix to make words meaning "one who", for example, er (teacher), etc.

6. Create lists of words that can be made from certain roots. For example, work- works, working, worked, worker.

7. Play 1 Minute Prefixes or Suffixes. Time it. Write the roots on the smart board first. Students have one minute to list as many words as possible by adding prefixes and suffixes to the root words.

PREFIX-SUFFIX FORMAT

Fold long ways, hot dog style:

Word	Root	Prefix	Suffix	Means

EASY START PREFIX LIST

PREFIXES

The Prefix	It Means	Example to Model
anti	against	antiwar
auto	self	autobiography
bi	two	bicycle, binocular, bifocal
cent	hundred	century, centigrade
deci	ten	decimal
dis	not, opposite	disagree, dishonest
in	not	inaccurate, inactive
im	not	immature, impossible
mal	bad	malfunction
sub	under	submarine, submerge
mis	bad	misbehave
multi	many	multicolored, multimillionaire
oct	eight	octopus, octagon
off	from	offstage
on	on	ongoing, onshore
over	too much	overpriced, overdo
para	beside	parallel, paraphrase
peri	around	periscope, perimeter
pre	before	precaution, preamble
post	after	postdate, postscript, postpone
pro	in favor of	pro-American
re	do again	redo, rewrite, reappear
re	back	repay, recall, recede
super	over	supervisor, superintendent
tri	three	triangle, tricycle
uni	one	unicorn
under	below	underweight
un	not	unhappy

Adapted from *Reading Teacher's Book Of Lists*, and my lists.

EASY START SUFFIX LIST
SUFFIXES

The Suffix	It Means	Example to Model
able	capable of	teachable, buildable
age	action or process	marriage, voyage
ant	one who	assistant
ar	one who	liar
arian	one who	librarian, historian
cle	small	icicle, particle
cule	tiny	molecule
er	one who	teacher, baker
ectomy	surgery-removes	appendectomy
ery/ry	work	bakery, dentistry
hood	state/quality	childhood
ing	material	frosting, bedding
itis	inflamed	laryngitis, arthritis
man	someone works with	mailman
ment	a thing	instrument ornament
ment	state or quality	amusement, puzzlement
less	lacking	friendless, childless
ling	tiny	duckling
ship	state of	friendship
er	more, comparing	smaller, taller, wider
ful	full of	thoughtful. wonderful
ness	quality of	happiness, kindness
ine	chemical	chlorine, caffeine
ology	science of	biology
or	one who	doctor, actor
phobia	fear of	claustrophobia
orium	place	auditorium
th	state or quality	warmth, strength, length
ern	direction	eastern, northern, western
s, es	plural	toys, foxes

Adapted from *Reading Teacher's Book Of Lists*, and my lists.

SYLLABLES

TEACH SYLLABLE RULES

TEACH

Tip #1: Every syllable has *only one* vowel sound.

1. **VCV**
   Usually divide after the consonant.

2. **VCCV**
   Usually divide between the two consonants.

3. **VCCCV**
   Usually divide after the first consonant.

4. **COMPOUND WORDS**
   Divide between the two words.

5. **PREFIXES AND SUFFIXES**
   Prefixes are their own syllables. *Suffixes* vary: ed is a separate syllable; y usually combines with the preceding consonant and is a syllable.

6. **LE AT THE END**
   Le usually combines with the accompanying consonant to make up a syllable.

7. **VOWELS**
   Bossy 'R': ar, er, ir, or, ur, are usually a syllable, and shouldn't be divided.

8. **DIPHTHONGS**
   oi, ou, ow, oy, oo, form one syllable.

9. **VOWEL (DIGRAPHS) TEAMS**
   ee, ae, ea, ai, oa, ay, and ue are each a syllable.

10. **Y AS A VOWEL**
    When y is a vowel, it is a syllable (As in city).

PRACTICE

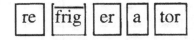

When teaching syllable rules, model writing each syllable in a box. Have students do the same. (See Syllable in a Box Reproducible, next page.)

TEACH OPEN AND CLOSED SYLLABLES

Syllables that end with a vowel are called *open* syllables. Open syllables usually end with long vowel sounds (me, open).

Syllables that end with a consonant are called *closed* syllables. Closed syllables usually have short vowels (pen, picnic).

PRACTICE

Open	Closed

Give students a list of words. Students underline closed syllables and circle open syllables (bug, garden, dog, kitten, me).

Chart open and closed syllables, while "Reading the Room" or in a list.

PRACTICE

SYLLABLE IN A BOX

EXAMPLE

e	lec	tri	ci	ty

TEACHING SENSATIONAL SYLLABLES

Seven sensational ways to teach students to find syllables:

Model (per each *beat*)

1. Clap hands

2. Stamp feet on floor

3. Blow puffs of air on palm of hand

4. Using fingers, (10 count); bump, or rap, on chin (underneath).

5. Ninja Know It All.

6. Wiggle hips, click fingers, click 'clickers', etc.

7. Tap the beat with pencil or chopsticks.

Teach students that each syllable has a vowel. Practice syllabic generalizations (prior page), dividing words into syllables.

Number The Beat

Make number signs (1-5) for each student (tagboard or laminated). Hold up a sign as you say a word: "How many beats, or syllables do you hear in this word?"

1	2	3	4	5+

Four Box Fold

1. (syll.)	2. (syll.)
3. (syll.)	4. (syll.)

Make up a chart or have students make 4 box paper fold (construction, plain or scrap paper). Students use counters to place in correct box matching the number of beats the words have (number of syllables). Teacher keeps checking.

Boxes With A Beat

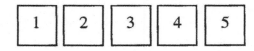

1	2	3	4	5

Students put down one finger in each box, matching the beats they hear (number of syllables).

Ninja Know It All Mini-Puppet

Take a loop (potholder kind); wrap it gently, not too tight, around your index finger to create the puppet's outfit. Draw a face on the back of your finger with marker. Use Ninja to divide between syllables. Model dividing a word on the board, or using wall print. Bring your finger straight down, slicing between each syllable. Say "Hi ya!" each time you make a division. As desired, students create their own puppets.

Use the Sensational Syllable Format on the next page. Have students record words under the correct column to reflect the number of syllables.

SENSATIONAL SYLLABLES FORMAT

1 SYLLABLE	2 SYLLABLES	3 SYLLABLES	4+ SYLLABLES

CONTRACTIONS

TEACH

A contraction is a short form of two words. An apostrophe is used in place of the letter or letters left out.

I am = I'm We are = we're	Chant the contractions from the accompanying lists. Start with easy to see 'contracting' words.
Exceptions	Teach can not (can't), will not (won't) later, as they are the exceptions to the Easy Start rule. "You take the letter out, then put the apostrophe in."

PRACTICE

1. Reading the Room print, point out contractions in the wall print or other. Frame or highlight them.
2. Find contractions in textbooks and other reading material.
3. Find contractions on a newspaper page or other print. Circle, underline, or put a triangle around them. List them.
4. Do a contraction fold (see next pages).
5. Give students a list, or do oral work or other to practice the two words contractions are made from, or make contractions from two words. Reverse contractions to two words and back to contractions.
6. Make up contraction games, chants, poems, cheers and songs.
7. Draw a contraction creation.
8. Create a contraction creation out of modeling compound or wax sticks.

Fastest to Start With Contractions			
I am	(I'm)	he is	(he's)
she is	(she's)	they are	(they're)
we are	(we're)	is not	(isn't)
would not	(wouldn't)	could not	(couldn't)

TEACHING COOL CONTRACTIONS

1. Introduce what the contraction looks and sounds like within a story or passage of text. (See Easy Start Contraction List.)

2. Model the contraction process, such as: I am= I'm; he is= he's; you are= you're.

3. Chant-"You take the letter out then put the apostrophe in" (use hand motions). I am ("take the letter out") = I'm (put the apostrophe in).

4. Find contractions in wall print and other (reading around the room).

5. Find contractions in books and other print.

6. Practice these teacher-shared ideas:
   - *Contraction Condo* (house)
   - *T-shirts*, (tops) or other self- checking center activity.

How To Make A Contraction Condo

Fold construction paper: Hot dog Fold, Hamburger Folds into rectangle open up, cut to folds, at middle. Model as you go.

Isn't		Is	Not
I'm		I	Am
He's		He	Is
We're		We	Are

(front folded)   (opened up)

Let students decorate with people, doors, windows, as desired.

How To Make The Shirts

Make a pattern of a shirt. Using the enclosed Easy Start Contraction List, make up a batch of tagboard or laminated tops. On the front list a contraction, on the back, the two original words. Using spring-type clothespins, and permanent markers write the words making up the contractions. Students match the pins to the front of the shirts, flip over to the back to self-check. Store in a small basket or baggie for center activity, or choice time, at desk.

Repeat—Repeat—Repeat

Use contractions in 'rounds', make up songs, write with them. Find more in wall and book print. Contractions are really cool!

OTHER CONTRACTION IDEAS:

EASY START CONTRACTIONS LIST

NOT:		**ARE:**	
aren't	are not	they're	they are
can't	can not	we're	we are
couldn't	could not	you're	you are
didn't	did not		
doesn't	does not	**HAVE:**	
hadn't	had not	I've	I have
hasn't	has not	they've	they have
haven't	have not	we've	we have
isn't	is not	you've	you have
mustn't	must not		
shouldn't	should not	**AM:**	
wasn't	was not	I'm	I am
weren't	were not		
wouldn't	would not	**IS:**	
		he's	he is
HAD:		here's	here is
he'd	he had	it's	it is
I'd	I had	she's	she is
she'd	she had	that's	that is
they'd	they had	there's	there is
we'd	we had	what's	what is
who'd	who had	where's	where is
you'd	you had	who's	who is
		let's	let us
WILL:			
he'll	he will		
I'll	I will		
it'll	it will	**EXCEPTIONS:**	
she'll	she will	won't	will not
there'll	there will	can't	can not
they'll	they will		
we'll	we will		
you'll	you will		

FLIP FLAP DECODING REVIEW

Colorful Compound Words	Colorful Compound		Two Words
Cool Contractions	**Contraction**		**Old Words**
Prefixes **Suffixes**	**P:** **S:**		

Sensational syllables	1	2	3	4+

Wow Words!	1. Word	2. Means	3. Sentence

Create your own, or use the Flip Flap Fold format on the next page.

FLIP FLAP FOLD
REVIEW REPRODUCIBLE

CUT	Fold back	
CUT	Fold	
CUT	Fold	
CUT	Fold	
	Fold	

1. Cut on dotted lines. Fold on top (over), to the right.
2. Match the folds. Use to review phonics rules, etc.

ZIG ZAG PATTERN
COMPOUND WORDS, CONTRACTIONS, SYLLABLES, PREFIXES & SUFFIXES

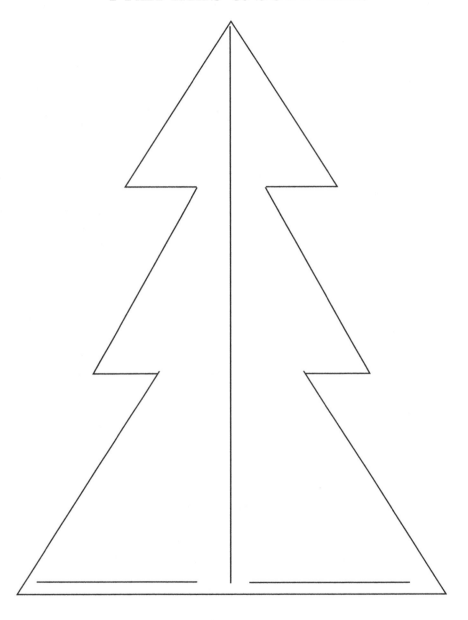

1. Make pattern on construction paper, tag board, or other stiff paper.
2. Cut the parts, like a puzzle.
3. Play matching games.

FOUR BOX FOLD

DECODING ACTIVITY

1	2	3	4
Examples: un teach tree I	happy er house am	*un*happy teach*er* treehouse I'm	Prefix Suffix Compound word Contraction

1. Fold 8 1/2 x 11 scratch paper into 4 boxes (either hot dog or hamburger fold).

2. Number 1, 2, 3, 4.

3. Call out prefixes, suffixes, compound words, and contractions. (See above model.)

Chapter 5
Reading Shortcuts and Interventions

Easy Start Ways to Fill in the Gaps

There are diverse voices in our classrooms. Meeting unique needs of Title I, second language, special needs and students who have fallen behind provides challenge for teachers., schoolhouse and home. In order to assist students with interesting yet effective lessons which promote success, strategies for differentiation and accommodations are vital.

In "double alignment" not only do students meet designated targets for skills mastery, but standards- based lessons must consider students' interests and their learning preferences.

This chapter offers classroom- tested ways to fill in learning gaps and move forward in skill acquisition. Think in terms of skills known and unknown, as measured by informal observation and assessment. Then teach faster, not slower, but repeat in a variety of brain- compatible ways.

Use interventions and shortcuts to accelerate basic skills instruction. Remember, noted brain researcher Robert Sylwester told us that "practice makes permanent". I really like that.

How to Correct 12 Common Word Recognition Problems
Reading Inventory and Errors (Miscues) Record
100 Multi-Sensory Literacy Strategies

EASY START INTERVENTIONS
HOW TO CORRECT 12 COMMON WORD RECOGNITION PROBLEMS

1. Word-By-Word Reading

- Provide reading material with easier skill level.

- Use familiar materials.

- Record the student's own stories or writing.

- Build sight vocabulary.

- Use pacing devices, mini flashlight, etc.

- Follow along with recorded stories.

- To determine if book is too challenging, at frustration level use the five finger technique. Put down one finger each time there is an unknown word. If student hits five, consider a lower difficulty level. Interest comes first., however.

- Model the reading, with *"echo" reading*. Teacher reads out loud; student follows, slightly behind.

- Use lots of practice, to build fluency.

- Teach students rate builders, to build speed.

2. Incorrect Phrasing

- May be caused by insufficient knowledge of the vocabulary, insufficient comprehension, or development of poor oral reading habits, from lack of practice.

- Build sight vocabulary.

- Follow along with audio books.

- Use lower skill level material.

- Model proper phrasing in the reading.

- Review punctuation marks—draw analogy between traffic signs and punctuation marks (eg. stop sign is a period).

- Reproduce reading passages so that they are divided into two or three phrases, such as: Juan and Pedro were on their way to the movies.

- Choral reading—reading out loud, together.

- Write sentences using crayons. Make each phrase a different color. After reading sentences in color, have students read them in black and white print.

- Have students read or sing songs using chanting or sing-song voice.

3. Guesses Words

- Circle or underline the guessed words, if okay to write in book, *or*, stick post-it on unknown words.
- Use context clues (words around the word).
- Use beginning sounds as hints.
- Use lower level reading material.

4. Consonants Unknown

- Flash cards with sound and picture.
- Tape record words and have students write letters they hear at beginning or end of word.
- Write words that begin with the letter(s).
- Games and activities, for repetition.
- Record the consonant letters with their sounds; students need a chart with corresponding letters to see as they hear.
- Tactile/kinesthetic approaches.
- Make phonics posters.
- Make blending wheels.

- Use a phonics phone (plumber's elbow, P -trap) to magnify the sound.

5. Unknown

- Flash cards as above, with vowel sounds.
- Games and activities.
- Vowel poster(s).
- Commercial charts.

6. Poor Pronunciation

- Use games and activities, for lots of practice and repetition.
- Have students build a list of words they are working on; keep a progress chart.
- Do *Impress Method*, with teacher reading orally and student following slightly behind. (Also called "echo" reading.)
- Practice necessary dictionary and glossary skills.
- Practice *word pairs* such as hit/ heat.
- Make recordings.
- Lots of oral reading practice, alone, with teacher, or study partner.

7. Omissions

- Omissions are words, letters, or phrases which are left out of oral reading (may be done with silent reading as well).

- Use a paper reading guide, or bookmark, to follow.
- Build sight vocabulary.
- Use a finger or pacer to follow along the line.
- Choral reading with class; *modeling*, by instructor.
- Tape record student's reading; play back (with written material in front of the student).

8. Repetitions

Student re-reads words or phrases.

- Use familiar material.
- Pacing devices.
- Read silently before orally.
- Record oral reading.
- Use hand or finger to pace.
- Do re-readings of the same material.

9. Reversals

- Student reads words from right to left instead of normal left to right sequence; example *was* for *saw*, or *pot* for *top*.
- Student reads letters in reverse, example *d* for *b*, or *p* for *g*.
- Student makes partial reversals in words, as *ant* for *Nat*.

- Student reverses words within sentences, as "The rat chased the cat", etc.
- Emphasize left to right in every-thing.
- Cover words or sentences with a card. Read the word or sentence as it is covered. Make a window marker; the line of print shows through the slot (tachistoscope).
- Pace reading with a left to right hand movement.
- Use flash cards.
- Trace challenging words. Use tactile, hands-on materials.
- Slow down reading if rushing.
- Use highlighting marker. Underline while reading (if possible).
- Use a magnetic board or felt letters., old time stuff, if available.
- Use a colored letter at beginning of confused letter.
- Use a sticky dot (colored) at the front of confused word(s).

10. Insertions

Student adds words which are not really in the sentence.

- Choral reading (out loud).
- Record oral readings.
- Point to each word as he/she reads.
- Lift a finger up and bring it down on each word as it is read.
- Work with comprehension strategies.

11. Substitutions

- Student substitutes one word for another.
- Make flashcards of challenging words.
- Work on beginning sounds or syllables that cause difficulty.
- Use the words giving difficulty in sentences.
- Choral reading.

- Read along with recorded passages.
- Practice with lots of repetition.

12. Sight Words

- Use tactile/kinesthetic techniques to learn new words (felt, velvet, salt, gelatin, corn meal, flour, sandpaper, etc.).
- Use pictures and configuration cues. (Monkey, for example). Flash cards, games and activities.
- Use high interest, low vocabulary reading materials.
- Use language experience stories.
- Use picture cards with word and picture.
- Pantomime certain words. Lots of practice.

Teach a consistent method to recognize unknown words

1. **Look at word.**
2. **See if any part of it looks like a word you know.**
3. **How does it begin? How does it end?**
4. **Read other words in the line and see what you think it should be.**
5. **Listen for the word in the rest of the lesson, and in other reading material**

EASY START READING INVENTORY

(Skill Levels 1–8+, or gaps)

Knows (+)	**Needs (-)**

1. Concepts about print   'Conventions'

2. *Word Recognition*

_____Letters/Alphabet   .... Letters

_____Phonemic Awareness   .... Sounds
                                                              .... Rhymes

_____Consonants   .... Initial
                                                              ....Medial
                                                              .... Final
                                                              .... Bossy 'R'
                                                              .... Blends
                                                              .... Digraphs
                                                              .... 'Special'—y, w, s

_____Vowels   .... Sounds
                                                              .... Rules
                                                              .... Digraphs
                                                              .... Diphthongs
                                                              .... Magic 'E'
                                                              .... Vowel Teams

_____Structural Analysis   .... Compound words
                                                              .... Contractions
                                                              .... Syllables
                                                              .... Roots
                                                              .... Prefixes
                                                              .... Suffixes

Knows (+)	Needs (-)

3. _____ Oral Reading

.... Pronunciation
...... (Errors Noted:)...Reversals
.... Insertions
.... Omissions
......................................Repeats
.... Punctuation
.... Phrasing
.... Expression

4. _____ Rate

.... Automatic
.... Fluent

5. _____ Vocabulary

...............................Sight Words
.... Synonyms
................................Antonyms
...............................Homonyms

6. _____ Spelling

....................................Syllables
.... Word Families
.... Basic Rules

7. _____ Comprehension

................................Main Idea
.... Details
.... Sequence
.........................Cause & Effect
.... Compare & Contrast
............................Other (Note)

EASY START ERRORS RECORD

The easiest marking system for miscues includes the following:

1. Hesitates: 'h'

2. Wrong word pronounced:
   write word said

3. Left out words, or parts of words:
   0 (circle)

4. Word-by-word reading:
   | | | (vertical lines)

5. Substitutions: write above the word

6. Insertions: insert word above sentence

7. Repetitions: wavy line shows repeated part

8. Reversals: write word reversed

9. Pronunciation: p

10. Guesses: underline guesses (or unknown) word

It is useful, when possible, to record the student's reading. Play back with reading material in front of the student. You might have the student record errors, using this method.
Depending on most frequently occurring miscues, practice intervention strategies. Be sure to chart student growth in skills mastered, reflect skills to master next.

GREAT REINFORCEMENT, INTERVENTION & PRACTICE ACTIVITIES!

1. Flip Card
Make a hinge on two 3" x 5" cards. Cut the top card shorter than the bottom. Draw or put a sticker on the top. On the inside (bottom card) print a blend or digraph. Students guess from the top card, then check inside.

2. Consonant Checkers
Find an old checkerboard. Laminate or cover with clear contact paper. Place a sticker on each of the red squares. Game is played by naming the beginning consonant of the sticker square landed on. Change stickers or drawings as frequently as desired to reinforce other word recognition skills.

3. Album Dictionary
Buy a cheap photo album (with self-sticking pages) to create an alphabet dictionary.

4 Vowel circles (Learning Circle)
Cut a 10" circle. Put stickers around the edge. Take spring-type-clothespins—put one vowel on each. Student attaches clothespin to the matching sticker's vowel sound.

5. Phonics Fun
Take empty t.p. or paper towel cardboard rolls. Cut in half, two parts. On one, print (or tape) consonants, such as C, B, M, T, H; on the other half put endings such as 'am', 'or', 'at' etc. Student holds the tops together & rotates, naming the words. Make as many as desired. Kids love these!

6. ABC Review Books
In one or separate books—do letters by attribute, alliteration, shape or action. Example—S is for silly! Alliteration activities are great.

7. Word Cube
Buy six or more small (one inch) wooden cubes (craft store). Write one word on each cube to create a sentence. Turn the cubes to another side and make up a new sentence. Suggestion, color code sentences with different color ink. Students put the sentences together to make sense.

8. Spelling Yarn Fun
Have class write words in glue on heavy paper stock (poster board). Then, use yarn to string the word. Turn this to a tactile adventure at desk or center, with students guessing each other's words.

9. Fortune Cookies!
Cut off the corner of an envelope to create a paper Chinese Fortune cookie. Hide the phonics surprise in the 'cookie' and tape it shut. Be sure cookie is folded into the traditional fortune cookie shape.

10. Sentence Strip Writing Practice
On half-size sentence strips, cover with contact paper, or laminate. Student has his/her own name/letter strip and wipe-off crayons for tracing practice at center or desk. Add wax sticks, (wikki sticks) or pipe cleaners and it's more tactile!

11. Sentence Strip Books
Make books from sentence strips. Staple word cards to each strip.

12. Alphabet Chips
Take large, old poker chips and put to a clever use. Attach one letter per chip. Store in a container to be used for letter recognition or sentence writing practice, at center or desk.

13. Sight Vocabulary
Write one new word or phrase to practice per card. Punch a hole in each, near the top. Hang on a shower curtain ring, for easy opening. Cards come on and off as mastered.

14. Tactile Ideas
Use the following kitchen items for students' practice tracing/writing words/ letters at desk or center: corn meal, salt, flour, glitter glue, Jell-O, sugar, corn starch, alphabet cereal. Each student works on a place mat, cookie sheet, or on a plastic cloth. Trace letters/words on feathers, pom poms, in the air, on a partner's back, on sandpaper, felt, sponge or foam pieces. Use a (new) toothbrush to trace on each other's backs.

15. Cereal Box Books
Put the notion of environmental print to work in your classroom. Each student makes a book from cereal box covers. Cover each page with contact paper. Bind with yarn. Put in library, center, or keep at desk. Find letters and words kids know.

16. Alphabet Board
Great center practice: put 26 library cards on a poster board, each labeled with an alphabet letter. Variations on this— students put sight words or letter cards in appropriate pockets. Can be self—checking.

17. Consonant Wipe-off Cards
Make a set of consonant cards on tag board; laminate for wipe-off crayons. Match upper and lower case letter, letter with picture, etc.

18. Tactile ABC
One letter per poster board, or piece of construction paper. Suggestions: create a *C* out of cotton balls and print 'cotton ball' underneath. *M* might be for macaroni, over the M, etc. (Yellow yarn in *Y* shape; dots pasted to a *D*, feathers as *F*, red hearts shaping *H*; etc.)

19. Paint Bags
Use a snack size or small zip lock bag and fill with two or more tablespoons of finger paint. Shut bag and reinforce with a heavy tape. This bag is great for writing, reading (and math) practice. Each student 'writes' with fingers or Q-tips. (Do check each bag for leakage when you make it). This is a *superb* tactile practice at center or desk.

20. Bean Alphabet
Use large lima beans to make a bean box or bag for each student. Write upper, lower case letter on each bean. Spray with clear acrylic (outdoors) to preserve. Students put together words and identify basic alphabet.

21. Rebus Sentences
Write rebus sentences as a model for students to read. Great way to start reading—kids love the rebus. Short stories can also be created.

22. Alphabet Dot To Dot
Take a piece of newspaper or other print; have student circle designated letters, vowels, blends, digraphs, etc. Or circle the as, b s, c 's etc. Color code, and connect the dots.

using markers or crayons. Great practice for alphabetical order or letter recognition.

23. "R" Controlled Vowel Match (Bossy 'R')

Take several small plastic Easter eggs. Label each with an R-Controlled vowel combination: ar, er, ir, or, ur. Cut small strips or circles and label each with a word using an R-Controlled vowel. Game is played by student matching the strip with the correct egg. Great review for center or desk, alone or with a partner.

24. Consonant Cards

Use poster board and make five large cards, one for each vowel. Print the vowel on the right side of the card. Make two slits on the left side of the card so that cardboard strips with consonants can be pulled through to create syllables. Use alone or with a partner.

25. Pop-Up Flash Cards

Use pop-up books idea to make a pop-up flash card. Write the new word on the outside with a picture clue inside. First, fold 5" x 8" index card in half. Next, cut two 1" parallel slits in the folded edge. Fold the cuts toward the open edge. Crease. Push the creased box into the inside opening. Open to pop up.

26. Flip Flap Books

Fold 9" x 12" paper into eighths; open up crease in middle and cut at center folds. For phonics practice, print a different letter on each flap, with the corresponding picture, inside. Also use for stories—character descriptions, sequencing.

27. Fish Fun

Learn spelling word(s) by fishing. Attach a paper clip to a paper fish. Attach a magnet to a string attached to a stick. Kids fish for spelling words, then read their catch and write a new sentence.

28. Tachistoscopes

a. Use a window (bill paying) enve—lope and cut the back off to reveal words. This technique assists word tracking.

b. Cut a window out of an index card.

c. "T.V." Tachistoscopes—In the center of a piece of cardboard, cut two horizontal slits about two inches apart, and wide enough to permit a two inch strip of stiff paper, or cardboard to slide through. The paper, as it is pulled through, exposes phrases or lines of print.

d. Cut a window in a strip of card—board wide enough to fold into a four inch wide sleeve. On another sheet of cardboard, slightly less than four inch wide, print sight words. Write the words three quarter inches apart, so they will show one at a time when inserted card is moved up or down.

29. Eggsactly Endings

Use plastic eggs to create egg word fun. On one half of each egg, write an ending. On the other half, write beginnings. As student turns the egg, say each word being formed.

100 MULTI-SENSORY READING STRATEGIES (With Pizzazz!)

1. Use a music box, train whistle, or play a recording, whistle, slide flute for subject transitions. Sing word or letter songs, as you make transitions.

2. For chalkboard practice, (old slates if you have) the students dip sponges or q-tips in water and write.

3. Make shadow puppets— use craft sticks and project these.

4. Color code punctuation and capitalization with colored markers or crayons. Use red for periods, yellow for commas, green for exclamation.

5. Have students practice counting by playing old fashioned jacks. Use activity with counting books, as Ten Apples On Top.

6. Say or sing the alphabet to a beat; use pop music. (Teach rote math tables to beat.)

7. Glue colored macaroni on craft sticks to make alphabet letters.

8. Teach new spelling words to music. Students spell the words, moving body parts to the rhythm.

9. Use flocked wallpaper samples for tactile tracing.

10. Make a flannel apron to turn yourself into a walking 'visual'.

11. Use puffy, colored pom-poms in varying colors and sizes as bingo manipulatives.

12. Use an indoor hopscotch pad so students move to learn spelling words. Or, use yarn, tape or rope to mark off the area. Take this activity outdoors, too.

13. Put Cheerios cereal on a pipe cleaner or piece of uncooked spaghetti to create an at-desk-counting unit (use with counting books).

14. Tape off your classroom floor to create temporary balance beams, shapes (such as circles and squares). Students walk on the lines feeling the shapes and gaining balance.

15. To make a dry-erase board, buy a large piece of masonite paneling at a local lumber yard. Cut it into lapboards.

16. Buy inexpensive magnetic photo albums to use as mini-centers. Fill with practice pages, stories, etc.

17. Teach spelling with alphabet cereal or macaroni. Students love to learn to spell in this tactile way.

18. Put an old bathtub, beanbag or child's wading pool in a corner of your classroom to create a reading center.

19. For very tactile students, if possible, have available an old exercise bike, typewriter, mini-trampoline, rocking chair to study on.

20. Use configuration cues, or use word pictures. Shapes provide strong visuals.

21. Place spelling words on large cards at eye level, to the left, in your room to serve as a strong peripheral visual.

22. Use modeling compound for tactile students to form letters and numbers. Also, wax sticks or pipe cleaners.

23. Use Velcro for lots of tactile strategies. Turn yourself into a visual with Velcro on an old shirt. Make a clock with Velcro clock parts.

24. Cut out giant sandpaper letters for students to trace and move around. (Center small size, or floor size.)

25. Use rebus activities for beginning reading practice.

26. Use small flashlights for tracking practice. Students follow along the line with their beam.

27. Use empty jars. Fill with spelling words Fill with spelling words, reading sequences, etc.

28. Use props of all sorts. Store in a toy box in the classroom, or at home.

29. Cut letters and shapes from sponges; moisten with water for boardwork or playground learning.

30. Wear a puppetry apron, with lots of pockets for surprises.

31. Use rolls of colored adding machine tape for reading, spelling practice, great for sequencing. String the colored rolls, when complete, around the room.

32. Hang mini - clotheslines of string; attach colored mini paper clips. Create vivid visuals (peripherals).

33. Use brain breaks at least every twenty minutes—stretching, aerobics moves; 'Finger Dance' at desk to *Flash Dance* tape, etc.

34. Use old games for a game center which reinforces literacy concepts.

35. Use beach balls, paddle balls, and hacky sacks for spelling practice. (Toss or roll back and forth, spelling out loud or to a partner).

36. Make up salt trays for tracing letters and numbers or practicing spelling (or flour, hair gel in baggie, etc.).

37. Cook. Read and do recipes.

38. Create student's private reading space with carpet squares or hula-hoops.

39. For a homemade abacus use hangers with clothespins. Even better, use colors, label with markers. Use with counting books; spelling.

40. Another classroom abacus idea—attach clothespins to chair backs.

41. Use rhythm instruments to do reading drill to a beat.

42. Use sentence strips (cut in half) at students' desks, for spelling practice.

43. Fold spelling words, sequences, geographical places, historical events, etc. into paper fortune cookies. Cut off the corner of each envelope; stuff with the fortune 'cookie' (or make real ones).

44. To create straight columns for doing math problems, turn notebook paper sideways (the lines are dividers). Tie in with reading activities.

45. Use body parts (length feet, fingers, etc.) to measure classroom items.

46. Use beanbags for perceptual practice. Tie in with rhythmic beat.

47. Overhead projector fun—students take turns creating letters, shapes, and num-bers with their fingers/hands.

48. Scratch and sniff learning fun for tactile students; write letters, words, numbers or math problems with glue on pieces of paper. Sprinkle with varying gelatin flavors.

49. Another fun picture clue—for teaching use of quotation marks, point out quote marks look like ears ("cc"). Ears hear what's said.

50. Buy inexpensive plastic mats for desk use. Perfect for all messy desk activities.

51. Send classroom texts and paperback books home in the larger size zip-lock bags.

52. To teach the days in each month to young students, have students make fists of both hands. The 'mountains' have thirty-one days, and the valleys are thirty (or less) days.   (Originator unknown.)

53. Use foods to teach shapes. Such as: circles (crackers, cookies, M&M's); squares (Wheat Thins); triangles (Doritos chips).

54. Use movement to teach punctuation. Run for exclamation; stop for period; pause, for comma.

55. To practice spelling in another tactile way, use finger paint or pudding.

56. Use alphabet cereal to teach alphabetical order.

57. Make jackets with marker or stick-on letters sold at stationery stores. Students form words with their bodies.

58. Get a hula-hoop. Tape numbers on the rim. Student standing in the hoop creates the times for class to guess.

59. Use post-it notes for students to write notes in their books. Or, colored tape flags.

60. Students can practice spelling, numbers and words using old cell phones.

61. Old cookie sheets are great for center or desk use. Provides tracing surface or keeping hands-on messy work in place. Also, useful for magnetic numbers and letters.

62. Tactile students trace letters, words, numbers, spelling in corn meal.

63. Take an old game like Racko and convert to alphabetizing practice. Or, create slot boards for alphabetizing practice.

64. Do shape writing, a good visual activity; have students turn their writing into the shape they are writing about. (Originator unknown.)

65. Movement fun—students move their bodies like magnets when studying magnets, growing plants when studying plants. Move like you are in space, etc.

66. Remember, paper bag puppets and finger plays for a visual.

67. For spelling practice fun, have your student/s write words on white construction paper with a white crayon. Paint over it, watch the magic!

68. Wear costumes depicting story or historical characters.

69. When teaching left and right concepts to young students, show them the 'L' the left hand makes with the index finger and thumb.

70. More magnetic photo album use—students can write over each plastic page. Use wipe-off crayons. Practice letters, words, spelling.

71. Play Baroque music, while students read and write.

72. Use active, inexpensive plastic toys and games to teach concepts. Use outgrown toys such as: bowling sets, sponge bats and balls, fishing poles, golf sets, Nerf balls, badminton and tennis, Velcro dart boards, etc. (Garage sales).

73. For novelty, use a remote controlled car in your classroom. Send messages and basic concepts around the room for learning fun!

74. Use a Kazoo band to accompany concepts taught through tunes. Students get to keep their Kazoos as a bonus.

75. Celebrate the end or completion of each unit or theme. Use a party theme, as possible have fun with streamers, horns etc. Maybe kazoos!

76. Play dough recipe:
    1/2 cup salt
    2 teaspoons cream of tartar
    1 cup water
    1 cup vegetable oil
    Food coloring
    Mix the dry ingredients, and stir.
    Cook mixture for two to three minutes; stir often.
    Knead the dough until it becomes soft and smooth.

77. Use butcher paper to create large story maps for classroom walls.

78. Do tongue twisters as a brain break and before oral reading or reports.

79. Here are favorite tongue twisters you might want to do word play with: "Double bubble gum bubbles double. Preshrunk shirts. Shy Sarah saw six Swiss wristwatches. Tie twine to three tree twigs. Fanny Fowler fried five fish for Francis Finch's father."

80. Use old newspapers, large construction paper, or butcher paper to create large letters and words. Fold into big letter shapes.

81. Make mobiles to reinforce vocabulary and comprehension.

82. Use conducting as an energizer or brain break. Play classical music. Have students conduct with arms, fingers, knees, eyes, toes.

83. Use toy (or real) keyboards or music apps to create rap and rhythm beats for reading and spelling activities.

84. Teach spelling and do phonics sounds practice while students are jumping rope.

85. Make surprise bags and boxes to teach concepts.

86. Class-size 'Oobleck' recipe for thirty students is:
    4 boxes cornstarch
    15 drops green food coloring
    Mix to even consistency.

Read *Bartholomew & The Oobleck* to accompany your experiments.

87. Use a metronome (as available, or a pencil or chopstick to add rhythm for spelling practice.

88. Use a lapboard (store bought or homemade), as a stage for puppets! A simple homemade board is easy to make from cardboard covered with contact paper. Make simple scenery or use other props.

89. Using flash cards, vary known and unknown words in the stack to ensure success. This is important to know.

90. Bring summer into your classroom with inner tubes, animal floats, etc. Students love to lounge and read during silent reading, etc. Also, why not a tiny tent or playhouse? (Home, too!)

91. Stick a cute sticker on the left side of each desk to show the side of the paper where writing should begin.

92. Cover a center table with clear contact paper and use wipe-off markers for loads of writing practice.

93. Practice spelling words on desks using a small amount of liquid bubble bath or detergent.

94. Tap out spelling words with rhythm sticks, pencils or chopsticks.

95. Place a red and green dot to show reversals.

96. Use magnetic tiles or index cards. Students line up letters to make words, or sentences.

97. For tracking (in reading), use discarded bill paying window envelopes.

98. For listening practice, tap out patterns for students to repeat.

99. Provide a clear acetate transparency if any old ones still in your supply stash. and washable marker. Place over textbook to work with the book without writing directly on it. Or use tracing paper and pencil.

100. Love!

OTHER GREAT IDEAS:

Chapter 6
Word Slingers

*Specific word learning and direct instruction
of vocabulary leads to improved fluency and comprehension.*

Types of vocabulary development include: listening, speaking, reading and writing. In order to improve students' vocabularies, most researchers state the importance of learning the meaning of words in a systematic fashion.

'Direct' teaching may consist of use of contextual clues, determining word origins, mastering roots, prefixes and suffixes and of course, engaging in daily oral, written and reading languaging opportunities. 'Indirect' vocabulary learning includes conversing with students, reading to students and wide independent reading enjoyed by students.

Vocabulary instruction aids fluency and reading comprehension. Teachers need concrete strategies for teaching specific words which may include using prior knowledge, advance organizers, context and other word learning strategies, including glossaries and reference aids. *Reading Champions!* activities included in Chapter 6 offer active engagement and extended vocabulary activities which benefit all students and help meet vocabulary concept development standards.

Vocabuary Builders and Boosters
Easy Start Word Bank
Graphic Organizers, Webs and Activities
Spell New Words Correctly
Multi- Sensory Reinforcement
Teach Possessives
Basic Grammar Review

INTRODUCTION TO CHAPTER 6

MODEL LOTS OF VOCABULARY WORD PLAY

WORD SLINGERS

VOCABULARY BUILDERS & BOOSTERS

The reading vocabulary of students grows at a rate of about 2,000 to 4,000 words per year, between grades 1-12. For grades 4-12, there is thought to be a 6,000 word gap in vocabulary size between a student at the 25th percentile and one at 50th percentile in vocabulary. Wide reading boosts vocabulary. There is a strong correlational relationship between vocabulary knowledge and comprehension, according to research.

Strategies—Know and Do

1. Keep a 'word bank' for each stu-dent, consisting of card file, folder, booklet, online record or other.

2. Write words on the wall. Keep a Word Wall going throughout the year. (*All skill levels*).

3. Teach words in and out of context.

4. Pre-teach vocabulary prior to reading, pull out and teach during the reading, then reinforce after, and keep using. Ask students to select their new, unknown, interesting,

fun to say or learn words before, during, and after reading.

5. *Immerse* the vocabulary words. Use *Novelty* to stand out.

6. Aim to teach five to ten words per day, fifty words per week, or more.

7. Teach the origins of words.

8. Make sure students can spell the new words.

9. Do some of the accompanying vocabulary strategies.

10. Use dictionaries and glossaries routinely.

11. Consider vocabulary building as word play.

12. Wide reading builds and boosts vocabulary.

Use enclosed formats as reproducibles for practice or have them enlarged to classroom poster size or anchor chart. Laminate to reuse.

EASY START WORD BANK

Aa	Bb	Cc	Dd
Ee	Ff	Gg	Hh
Ii	Jj	Kk	Ll
Mm	Nn	Oo	Pp
Qq	Rr	Ss	Tt
Uu	Vv	Ww	Xx
Yy	Zz	Name:_____ Week:_____	

EASY START VOCABULARY BUILDER #1

1. NEW WORD	2. MEANS	3. SENTENCE
1		
2		
3		
4		
5		
6		
7		
8		
9		
10		

EASY START VOCABULARY BUILDER #2

WORD / PHRASE	DEFINE IT	SENTENCE	SYNONYM / ANTONYM	PART OF SPEECH	DRAW IT
1.					
2.					
3.					
4.					
5.					
6.					
7.					
8.					
9.					
10.					

VOCABULARY PRACTICE

Pad & Pencil Activity

Keep a pad of paper by your book or device. List new words and the page number. After you finish reading the sentence, paragraph, or page, look them up, and use often. *Or* use this format.

List *new* words, *interesting* words, *cool* words, *fun-to-say* words, words you have seen before but are not sure of.

Word	Page
1. _____	_____
2. _____	_____
3. _____	_____
4. _____	_____
5. _____	_____
6. _____	_____
7. _____	_____
8. _____	_____
9. _____	_____
10. _____	_____
11. _____	_____
12. _____	_____

Now, go back and pick *five* words. Web them. (See next pages).

VOCABULARY BOOSTERS CHART

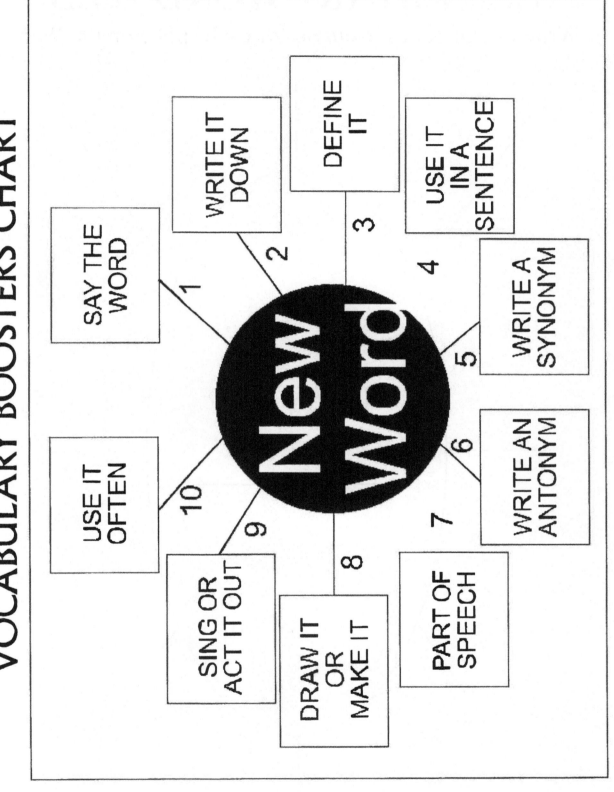

EASY START WORD WEB

Write or call out a *Synonym* for each spoke on the Web.

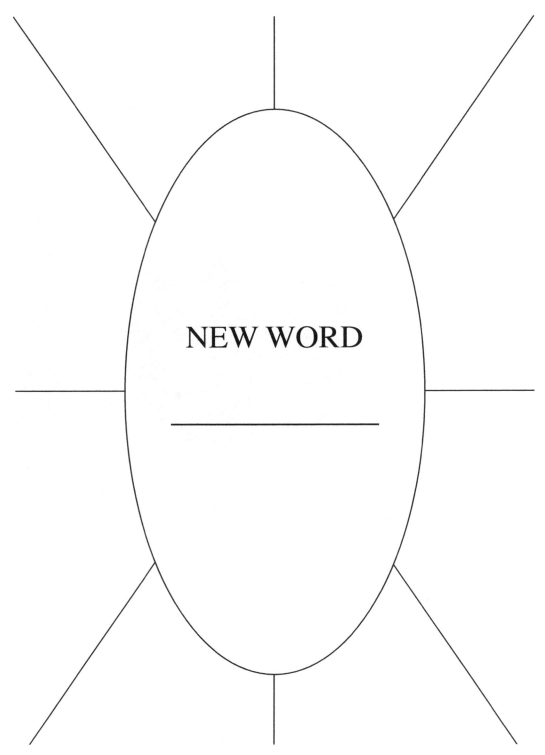

NEW WORD

Use as Anchor chart or smart board or other.

VOCABULARY PRACTICE

A. **Bookmark Vocabulary**: Cut up tagboard, construction, or other stiff paper into bookmarks. They should be plain on both sides; length is optional. Pass out a stack to each student. Tell students to fill the bookmark with new words and corresponding page numbers, as they read.

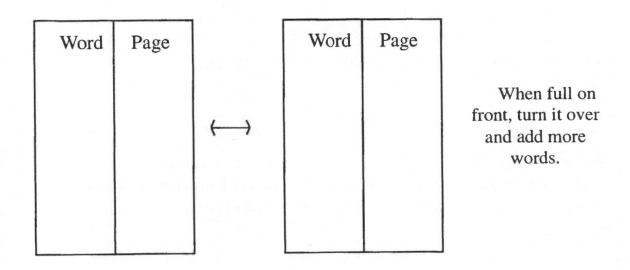

When full on front, turn it over and add more words.

Say: "Just keep reading. Don't stop to look up the words until one side of the bookmark is full." Do a web or other vocabulary activity with selected new words, after bookmark is full on both sides. Practice the new words-individual, whole class, partners or teams.

MORE VOCABULARY PRACTICE

B. **Flashcard Pack** : Pass out a stack of index cards (small sizes best, to 'shuffle the deck') to each student. Rubber band the stack. Put one new word on each card. On the front of the card write the word in the middle, page number in a corner, then continue reading. When finished with sentence, paragraph, or page, look up the word. On the back, write the definition, use it in a sentence, etc. (Web activities.)

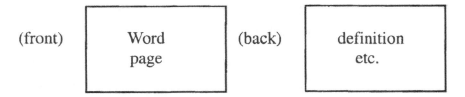

Use like flashcard packs. Practice alone, in pairs or teams.

C. Pass out a large (plastic) shower curtain ring to each student (These are easier to open than the small metal ones). Provide stacks of small hole punched cards. New words are added to the ring stack. Take off the word cards when mastered.

D. Whichever method you use with your student or class, practice the new words, and use
oft in conversation and writing activities. Have students practice with each other, in pairs. Practice in short increments. Check students' cards to ensure correct spellings.

FAVORITE WORDS
VOCABULARY BADGES
This is a fun activity, or series of activities.
"What's the word?" "What does it mean?"

At a stationery or office supply store, buy a box of name badges: pin-on badges, or around-the-neck types (pin-ons are cheaper than the around the neck kind). Pin-on type are re-usable by inserting scratch paper inside.

(Front)

Read

Reader

(Wear around neck type)

(Back with pin)

There are several ways to use vocabulary badges in your class.

1. Students select their favorite word of the day, and draw it and write it on their badge. Go around the room and have students call out their favorite word for the day, which they are wearing. List on the wall (butcher paper) or write on smart board. Select one to three of the class' favorites and Web or other.

Use as many of the class' words as possible throughout the day.

2. Play charades - act out favorite words for the day.

3. Do something fun to reinforce favorite words. Make up songs using the words, draw them, do chants with them, create words in clay, or wax sticks (create symbol of each word). Write, using the favorite words.

NEW WORD FORTUNE COOKIE

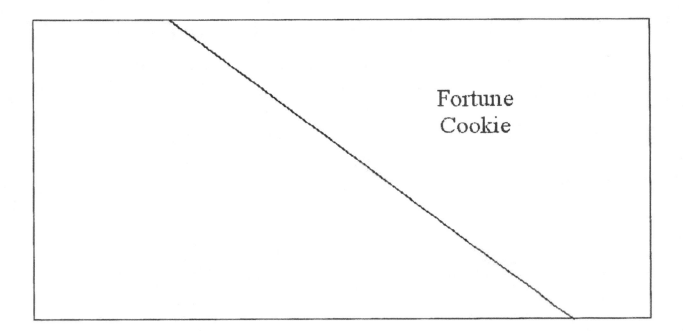

1. Cut corner of envelope.
2. Fold up into fortune cookie.
3. Students hide one new word, per cookie.
4. Place fortunes into large size Chinese food container.
5. Web the new words, or other activity.

SPELL NEW WORDS CORRECTLY

What you Need To Know

Almost 85% of English follows consistent patterns and rules. To

successfully teach spelling, teach the structure of the language.

Sounds—Sounds are represented by letters.

Syllables—Words are made of syllables (every syllable has a vowel or 'y').

Generalizations and rules—Use high utility, which (generally) work.

Word Families—37 word families make over 500 words.

What Works / How To

A. Teach rules that apply.

1. 'Q' is always followed by 'U' (queen). (Q & U get 'married' .)
2. Soft g (George) and c (city) are followed by i, y, or e.
3. Use dge after short vowels (ridge) and ge after long vowels (page).
4. Usually words end in le not el (tumble).
5. After a short vowel, put a t before ch (stretch).
6. If a word sounds like/ but f is wrong, use ph (phone) or sometimes gh (cough).
7. Occupation words end in er, (teacher), or (doctor).
8. Add a prefix to a root word; the root stays the same, (ex- ample misspell.)
9. Change y to i, when adding a suffix, where y is preceded by a consonant. (silly-sillier).
10. To make a word ending in y plural, change the y to i and add es (baby-babies).

B. Practice out, and in text.

1. 'Spell the room'.

2. Find the elements in books.

3. Do mini-lessons on the rules.

C. Use correct models, all the time.

1. Teacher models. Students practice.

2. Skip scrambled words, word searches, crossword puzzles.

3. Post (on boards, walls) *only* correct models. Avoid publishing "Inventive Spelling" on papers, or stamp Draft.

D. Use strategies that work.

1. Spell and Check (enclosed).

2. 'Triple S' Spelling Success Strategy (enclosed).

3. Letter tiles, cubes etc. (manipulatives).

4. Paper Plate Spelling (enclose).

5. Spelling Patterns (word families).

6. Word Banks (enclosed).

7. Word Walls

E. Tips and Secrets.

1. Practice frequently with lots of repetition.

2. Use Vocabulary Boosters Chart *(*enclosed) consistently.

3. Do a variety of activities, chants, and games.

4. Avoid all competition in spelling.

5. Instruct in a multi-sensory mode.

6. Teach spelling as *thinking* and *word construction*.

7. Have fun with origins of words.

8. Proofread and correct spelling errors.

9. Use dictionaries and glossaries routinely, every day.

10. *Read* widely; *write* to reinforce.

11. Teach spelling mini-lessons, daily or bi-weekly.

PRACTICE

SPELLING REINFORCEMENT-MULTI-SENSORY IDEAS

1. Teach new spelling words to mu-sic; students move body parts to the varying rhythms.

2. In addition to Word Wall(s), place spelling words on large cards and place at eye level in the room.

3. Trace spelling words (with fingers) on sandpaper or felt.

4. Write words on white construction paper with white crayon. Paint over it; watch the magic.

5. Sing the spelling words.

6. Chant the spelling words.

7. Use a metronome to add rhythm for spelling practice.

8. Toss a nerf ball or stuffie around, as words are spelled.

9. Make a clay model of favorite words.

10. Wear a word badge to help remember the spelling (enclosed).

11. Jump rope while spelling the word(s).

12. 'Rap' the spelling word(s).

13. Spell out a word as you go under a limbo jump rope.

14. Students toss a bean bag, ping pong ball or Koosh ball back and forth as they spell out words.

15. Break up spelling lists into chunks; instead of teaching twenty spelling words per week, master *five* spelling words per day.

Your Ideas

TOP TEN SPELLING SECRETS ACTIVITY

1. 'Q' is always followed by 'U' (queen). (Q & U get 'married').

2. Soft *g* (George) and *c* (city) are followed by *i, y*, or *e*.

3. Use *dge* after short vowels (ridge) and *ge* after long vowels (page).

4. Usually words end in *le* not *el* (tumble).

5. After a short vowel, put a *t* before *ch* (stretch).

6. If a word sounds like *f* but *f* is wrong, use *ph* (phone) or sometimes *gh* (cough).

7. Occupation words end in *er*, (teacher), *or* (doctor).

8. Add a prefix to a root word; the root stays the same. (example mis*spell*.)

9. Change *y* to *i*, when adding a suffix, where *y* is preceded by a consonant. (silly-sillier).

10. To make a word ending in y plural, change the y to *i* and add *es* (baby-babies).

Words

Rule 1:_____

Rule 2:_____

Rule 3:_____

Rule 4:_____

Rule 5:_____

Rule 6:_____

Rule 7:_____

Rule 8:_____

Rule 9:_____

Rule 10:_____

1. Use as a wall chart, boardwork, or other. Practice.
2. Students list as many words as possible, matching each rule.

TOP TEN SPELLING SECRETS

1. 'Q' is always followed by 'U' (queen). (Q & U get 'married').

2. Soft 'g' (George) and 'c' (city) are followed by 'i', 'y', or 'e'.

3. Use 'dge' after short vowels (ridge) and 'ge' after long vowels (page).

4. Usually words end in 'le' not el (tumble).

5. After a short vowel, put a 't' before 'ch' (stretch).

6. If a word sounds like 'f' but 'f' is wrong, use 'ph' (phone) or sometimes 'gh' (cough).

7. Occupation words end in 'er', (teacher), or (doctor).

8. Add a prefix to a root word; the root stays the same. (example misspell.)

9. Change 'y' to 'i', when adding a suffix, where 'y' is preceded by a consonant (silly–sillier).

10. To make a word ending in 'y' plural, change the 'y' to 'i' and add 'es' (baby–babies).

PRACTICE SPELL & CHECK

1. Fold construction or (recycled) 8 1/2 x 11 paper into thirds (Hot dog folds). Start with "Fold to the middle". Model folding to three columns. Number the columns, 1, 2, and 3.

2. Student WRITES word in middle column. Make sure it is *correctly* spelled to start. Double check the model. Have kids look at each others' papers to make sure word is spelled correctly.

3. Student PICTURES word; eyes closed, or look up to the left for recall (especially if right handed).

4. Student COVERS word by folding over right hand flap.

5. Student WRITES the word from memory in the left side column.

6. Student opens, CHECKS and corrects if necessary by looking at original word in middle. (*Make sure it is correctly spelled to start with.*) If a letter or letters are missed, write word again, correctly, three times. Make the missing letters *stand out*.

7. Students may practice with each other, or at home. Practice daily, as often as possible.

1. Left Flap	2. Middle	3. Right Flap

TRIPLE 'S' SPELLING SUCCESS STRATEGY

(Adapted by Rita Wirtz; from NLP-Neuro Linguistics)

WHAT TO DO

1. If one letter (or more) is incorrect, do some of the helpful hints listed next.

2. Place correct spelling of word above student's eye level to *left* (or *right*, if left-handed). Use scratch paper, index card, etc.

3. Have student picture the correct spelling. Break the word into two or three chunks, if a long word. Look at the number of letters above and
below the line. Notice whether there are 'loops' or flags, etc.

4. Trace the letters in the air with two fingers, nose, eyes, foot, elbow, etc.

5. Have student write down the spelling on the card or paper. Check it, for correctness.

HINTS

1. Tell the student to picture the word or letters in a favorite color or cartoon. Make letters stand out—bigger, brighter, closer, different color, etc.

2. Put letters on top of a favorite picture of someone/something.

3. Make letters smaller or in a different shape, add happy face, etc. On double letters, or letters that do not sound like they look, make these stand out.

4. Tell student to pretend his/her eyes are a camera—make a clicking sound and do with fingers, as if taking a picture of each letter. Example- *read*: *r* (click), *e* (click), *a* (click), *d* (click). Pretend you are a camera. (Depending on grade level.)

P.S. This works because spelling is in part, very visual and often can't be remembered through sounds only. Adding tactile/kinesthetic activities makes this a wonderful multi-sensory method. For older students, omit the camera click. Have them just look at the word, hold up at or above eye level. This imprints correctly, in the brain.

PAPER PLATE SPELLING DRILL

This is a perfect multi-sensory d1ill which involves the whole class. You can do variations of this Spelling Drill by practicing roots, prefixes and suffixes, inflectional endings, and compound words and contractions. Punctuation paper plates can also be made and added to the d1ill. Make sets of capitals or lower case.

Paper Plate Spelling is fun and the kids love to do this! Make two sets of alphabet plates, (plain white, cheap plates work great) or one set of alphabet plates, plus additional set of vowels. Pass around the plates. Tell students they will come up to the front of the room when they have the letters you call out, and the first student up stays up. (Be sure to stress good manners, sharing turns up.) Model first. Make sure every student gets a turn. Call out a spelling word, or a new sight word you are studying. As you call out each letter, a student holding that letter comes up; students get in correct order of the spelling. Hold plates out high enough for whole class to see. Then everyone chants the spelling: R-E-A-D spells READ, etc. Reminder, this strategy can also be used to practice inflectional endings, compound words, roots, prefixes and suffixes, and contractions.

(Add er, ing, s, re- Reader, Reading, Reads, Reread)
(Add un; change to happier, happiest, etc.)

YOUR IDEAS:

TEACH POSSESSIVES

Tip: (Possessives link grammar with spelling)

TEACH

POSSESSIVES SHOW OWNERSHIP

Singular Possessive

To make the possessive of a singular word or name, add an apostrophe and an *s* ('s): (Paula's book, the girl's dress).

Plural Possessive

To make the possessive of a plural word ending in *es*, or a singular word ending in *s*, just add an apostrophe: (girls' dresses; cats' toys; James' cars).

PRACTICE

1. "Read the Room", looking for possessives in the wall print.

2. Point out possessives in books, reading material of all sorts.

3. Be sure to model each type

4. Use possessives routinely in class work.

5. Act out the possessives.

6. Have kids practice chants for possessives.

7. Play games, do chants, make up cheers. Get silly.

8. Pass a Koosh ball around, saying a possessive each turn.

9. Do the limbo, saying a possessive each turn going under the jump rope. Play music. (old Limbo Rock would be fantastic).

10. Let students teach each other the possessive rules.

11. Practice daily, as often as possible.

12. Look for possessives in students' writing. Make sure they are correct.

TIP: Make sure kids know the difference between contractions and possessives. They mix these up constantly. Differentiate between them clearly, as often as possible.

GRAMMAR COUNTS

REVIEW BASIC ENGLISH GRAMMAR
SHORT MINI-LESSONS

1. Find as many adjectives (nouns, verbs, etc.) as possible on page.

2. Describe a dangling participle. Find one in your writing, and correct it. (Optional!)

3. Find out how to diagram sen-tences. Then practice it.

4. Proofread someone else's paper, then discuss the errors and changes.

5. Study an old-fashioned grammar book. Master a rule or concept every day. (As possible)

6. Write on designated topic for five minutes, using as many adjectives (etc.) as possible. Chart growth.

7. Describe the major grammar elements. Write one example per index card. Stack of flashcards. Side 1: what it is (adverb, etc.). Side 2: the word itself. Practice with partners.

8. Make grammar charts to hang around the room.

9. Correct grammar in students' work. Better, have kiddos do theirs.

YOUR IDEAS:

FIND THE NOUN GAME

Person	Place	Thing

1. Find examples of as many parts of speech as possible in
   your book.
2. Adapt format to other parts of speech.
3. Review parts of speech

Chapter 7
How Reading Champions Read Non-Fiction

Good readers use specific strategies to find meaning

State standards and frameworks stress the importance of purposeful reading to determine meaning. "Students read and understand grade-level appropriate material. They draw upon a variety of comprehension strategies as needed... e.g., generating and responding to essential questions, making predictions...." (California State Standards)

Research tells us that good readers are purposeful and actively engaged with text. Understanding can be readily improved by direct instruction hat helps readers use a wide variety of strategies. Put Reading First "National Institute for Literacy) suggests six techniques with a scientific basis for improving comprehension: monitoring comprehension, metacognition (thinking about thinking), using graphic organizers, generating and answering questions and summarizing.

Effective comprehension instruction which helps students meet standards includes direct teaching and modeling, guided practice (directed reading activities) and transfer or application activities. Reading Champions! offers teachers ready to use tools for their 'toolboxes' and translates research into everyday routine.

Structural Features of Text
Teach What Reading Champions Do
Easy Start Content Reading List
Practice Rate Builders to Build Comprehension
Directed Reading Activities and Content Mini- Lessons

Predictions, Questions, and Responses

INTRODUCTION TO CHAPTER 7
MASTER TEXTBOOKS (NON-FICTION)

Some textbooks are easier to read than others. There are several reasons, including the following:

- Unknown general vocabulary

- Unknown technical vocabulary

- Inconsistent author's pattern (main ideas throughout book)

- Unclear organizational structure (compare and contrast, cause and effect, etc.)

- Layout is inconsistent

- Long and boring (to students)

In this section you learn how to read for information

1. Teach a basic "Book Walk". (enclosed)
2. Practice rate builders to boost comprehension.
3. Follow the layout of a book.
4. Ensure learning, remembering and recall.

NON-FICTION SUCCESS SECRET
Teach What Reading Champions Do

Before Reading	During Reading	After Reading
Purpose for Reading 'Walk-through' Make Predictions Web Chapter Titles Skim/Scan Author's Pattern Vocabulary List Graphic Organizers	Ask Questions More Predictions Reread Vocabulary List Adjust Rate Take Notes Summarize Graphic Organizers	Retelling Summarizing Rereading Graphic Organizers Inferences Quick Writes Make New Predictions Teach Someone Else
What do you already know? What do you need to know? Why do you need to know this?	What are you reading? What have you learned already? Retell what you've read so far.	What did you learn from the reading? What will you read next to learn more? Will you recommend this material to others?

EASY START CONTENT READING SKILLS LIST

Word-Meaning Skills
(Vocabulary)

1. Understand terms related to the subject.
2. Use the dictionary.
3. Use new words in speaking and writing.
4. Understand roots, prefixes, and suffixes.
5. Understand figurative language.

Comprehension Skills

1. Recognize and understand main ideas.
2. Recognize relevant details.
3. Organize ideas in a sequence.
4. Distinguish between fact and opinion.
5. See cause and effect.
6. Evaluate what is read.
7. Make generalizations and draw inferences based upon the facts.

8. Make predictions.
9. Read widely, additional same topic references.

Study Skills

1. Be familiar with many sources of information.
2. Use dictionary, encyclopedia, thesaurus, etc., efficiently.
3. Read maps, graphs, and tables.
4. Set purposes for varying types of reading.
5. Survey materials before reading.
6. Adjust rate of reading speed to the purpose and content.
7. Construct an outline and use other graphic organizers.
8. Summarize information read.
9. Memorize, using time-tested strategies.
10. Overlearn the information.

STUDENT FOCUS AREAS:

RATE BUILDER CHART

1. *Sit up straight, feet flat on the floor.*

2. *Hold book up, in your hands, or on desk, at 45 degree angle. This helps you see more print.*

3. *Do a visual exercise before you start.*

4. *Use your index finger as a pointer.*

5. *Practice rapid page turning.*

6. *Skip the little words.*

7. *Stay away from the margins.*

8. *Use a metronome to speed up.*

9. *Use your strategies to master them.*

10. *Practice reading faster every day.*

PRACTICE RATE BUILDERS TO ENHANCE COMPREHENSION

There are two types of reading, or reasons to read:

1. Reading For Information, and
2. Reading For Enjoyment.

When you read for information, the faster you read, the better your comprehension, and more time for *syntopic* or same topic reading. When reading for enjoyment, no speed drills, as speed is not the essence, pleasure is. Savor it, more slowly. Every word may be important, and one word may change the meaning.

TIPS

1. Practice the accompanying rate drills, every day.

2. Practice *skimming* and *scanning* and *dipping* throughout the day, including mini-lessons. In skim-ming, the reader looks quickly down the page, in a global, yet linear way. Skimming can also be done by looking at first lines of the paragraph, or last, or skimming through the Author's Pattern (enclosed).

3. In scanning, the reader looks for a very specific thing—a fact, detail, etc. The reader dips in to find the specific information.

It is critical to do the following when reading non-fiction of any type:

1. Do KWLW (KW parts) to connect information with what you know and want to know.

2. Have a purpose for the reading. Why do you need to read this? What do you need to find out?

3. Make predictions about the reading.

4. Ask questions.

5. Skim and scan.

6. Use strategies to organize information.

THOUGHTS AND IDEAS

RATE BUILDING PRACTICE
RESEARCH & CLASSROOM TESTED TECHNIQUES

Learn To Read, Read To Learn, for syntopic (same topic) reading. Perceptual number of letters your eyes can perceive and understand in a single sweep; the greater span of perception, the more you can read in a single glance. Most readers have a perception span of about 20 letters about four words.

1. For eye exercises, hold an unsharpened pencil (or pen) in front of you. Focus on a single letter. Move the pen or pencil toward you until the letter is a blur, move it away again. Do this 3 times. Or run your eyes up and down any corner of the room. (Helps tracking.)

2. Do 'seeing the room'—side to side eye sweep, first left side of room, then right.

3. Hold index fingers up in front of you, moving out to sides. Peripheral vision builder. (To see more print in a glance.)

4. Practice to see more words in one eye stop. (The more eye stops, the slower the reading.)

5. Do Tri-Focus practice—Read It Fast Drill. (Read the *s.) (From Steve Snyder and other originators.) See next page for format.

6. 'Tangerine' effect—look over book using soft focus.

7. Focus right above line of print. (Like reading the white space between the lines).

8. When you encounter two words together, focus on a spot in the middle of the line. Example (two words) information*explosion; example (three words)–future*information*explosion

9. Look at open book, at center crease. See all 4 corners of the book. Soften your gaze. (So lines of print aren't in hard focus). Instead, notice empty margins and white space between paragraphs. *Imagine an x connecting the 4 corners of the book.*

10. Super Dip—Quickly move eyes down center of page, in each paragraph.

11. Criss Cross: Scan top left corner to bottom right corner. Scan top right corner to bottom left corner.

12. Use a Metronome. Keep increasing your rate. (Purchase from a music store.) *Or* tap a pencil or chopstick.

13. Practice five to ten minutes per day, every day.

Knowledge Is Power!   Empower Yourself!

Adapted from *Brain Gym, Breakthrough Rapid Reading, Power Reading* and *Photo Reading* (Learning Strat. Corp.)

READ IT FASTER PRACTICE

```
*              *              *
      ➜              ➜
*              *              *

*              *              *

*              *              *

*              *              *

*              *              *

*              *              *

*              *              *

*              *              *

*              *              *

*              *              *
```

READ THE STARS OVERHEAD

Move your eyes across the page, then down. Read the stars across in each row until you reach the bottom. Next, apply this technique to other reading material. (Or enlarge to chart size, and laminate to poster size).

EASY START COMPREHENSION BOOSTERS
Teach Comprehension Fundamentals

12 Tips to Understanding
1. Have a purpose to read.
2. Connect with prior knowledge.
3. Predict and anticipate what it's about.
4. Find the main ideas.
5. Note important details.
6. Determine the sequence.
7. Compare and contrast it.
8. See cause and effect.
9. Organize the information.
10. Increase reading rate
11. Recall the information.
12. Apply, use the information *and* be sure to build vocabulary.

Easy Start Teaching
1. Practice Understanding: Use the accompanying Venn Diagram, Web, and other organizers.
2. Purpose: (Get started) Have a reason to read, a need to know. Ask questions. Make predictions.
3. Main Ideas: (Practice Tips)
   - What is the topic sentence?
   - What is the author's main point?
   - Find the main ideas.
   - Express the main idea in your words (out loud or written).
   - Put a post-it note on top of each main idea in textbooks (underline where possible).
4. Details: (Practice Tips)
   - Look for signal words which show importance, as "most important", etc.
   - Note when author spends a lot of time on one idea, or one specific fact, more than others.
   - Note captions, italics, bold, photos, headlines.
   - Look for important words at the end of sections or chapters.
   - Question at lower end of *Bloom's Taxonomy,* (Basic Bloom's enclosed) knowledge and comprehension levels; do get recall of certain facts, before moving up the hierarchy.
5. Sequence: (Practice Tips)
   - What happened first?
   - What happened next?
   - Read main ideas to get overview of sequence.
   - Enumerate (list) steps of a process, or chain of historical events.
   - Watch for signal words—"such as", "then", "finally", "second", "another", etc.
   - List a chain of events.
   - Note the steps in a proper order.

Tips: Grounding-Make sure students are on the correct page, and line. Say "Put your finger on ... "
Study: Place a clear transparency (acetate) over textbook; write on..
Look Backs: Tell students to look back in text if unsure of an answer.

DIRECTED READING ACTIVITY
12 Steps to Boosting Comprehension
Model and practice these strategies with your class

1. Do KWLW and a Book or Article Walk before you start reading.

2. Have a purpose for your reading.

3. Think about what you already know about the topic.

4. Predict what it's about, and what is going to happen, then keep checking on yourself.

5. Ask questions about what you read, after finishing a sentence, paragraph, or page.

6. Clarify or further explain what you're reading, while you're reading.

7. Sequence the events in chronological order.

8. Summarize out loud, by retelling in your own words what happened.

9. Write down the big ideas and several details.

10. Use graphic organizers to structure your thinking (sample formats, see pp.).

11. Read something else about the subject, to compare and contrast.

12. Teach this material to someone else.

Thoughts and Ideas

CONTENT AREA MINI-LESSON

Directed Reading Activity (DRA)
Using A Content Area Textbook

STEPS

1. Do KWLW first (p. to find out what students know. This should be fast! Check it out, then start the skills. RELATE ALL TEACHING TO BACKGROUND EXPERIENCE AS THE HOOK OR BUILD BACKGROUND EXPERIENCE.

2. Ask questions to clarify responses to the *K* and *W* portions of KWLW (Know, Want To Know) process (enclosed).

3. Introduce concepts and vocabulary necessary to understand the subject matter of the lesson.

4. Write the new words on the board, chart, or enclosed vocabulary formats (enclosed).

5. Make sure to motivate students about the subject and get their attention.

6. Direct silent reading. Have a purpose for the reading. Use formats to do the predictions (enclosed).

7. Ask question or questions to guide the reading. Use Four Big Ideas (p. or other way of organizing the students' thinking during silent reading.

8. You may want to do a Book, Chapter or Article Walk (enclosed).

9. Tell students to read to find the answer or answers to your question(s). Your question(s) may be based on a sentence, page or paragraph.

10. Discuss the students' responses. Were their predictions accurate?

11. Clear up any vocabulary or comprehension confusion or problems.

12. Oral reading or rereading of critical portions of text (re: skills work). Group choral response is appropriate.

THEN

Practice, to review all basic skills and ensure remembering. When you teach the skills isolated (detached) as Monday review one thing, Tuesday, etc., be sure to put everything back together so the students are not stuck in isolated pieces of learning.

If students appear to have mastered something, fine, but don't assume it is really totally learned. Reminder about the Ebbinghaus curve of forgetting: most information is forgotten within 24 hours, so a cycle of Review, Repeat, Application is a great way to teach or re-teach fundamental skills, whether decoding, comprehension, or vocabulary, or subject matter itself. Review at thirty minutes, four hours, 24 hours, etc.

A typical mini-lesson (fifteen-twenty minute chunks) may consist of the following activities:
- word recognition skills review
- developing basic subject matter concepts
- enlarging vocabulary
- practicing reading comprehension strategies

Select the particular activities appropriate to lesson time frame and students' need area(s).

Your basic goal for the Easy Start DRA should be that students recognize all the words they are reading, with complete understanding of the content as well. Obviously, the reading lesson should be at an instructional rather than frustration level. Be sure to model everything you want students to know and do, before they are expected to do the same strategies without help. Practice!

Things to Include

First of all, what should students know? What do they need to know to master the cognitive content? This determines what you should teach. In addition to pursuing the content, here are possible comprehension skills areas to focus on until the class is all at mastery levels:

1. Making predictions and having a purpose to read. Develop questions to look for.
2. Following directions (the linear way of doing things correctly, listening and 'attending' to task).
3. Recognizing the main idea or ideas (the key big idea/s of the information).
4. Noting the details (factual data, including details that explain, clarify, illustrate further, or describe).
5. Organizing the ideas (seeing the relationships among the ideas, grouping by attributes).
6. Determining the sequence (may be order of steps of a process, events, etc.).
7. Knowing the meanings of words. A reader's vocabulary is dependent on his/her background experience and level of information about the subject. Wide reading builds vocabulary.

DIRECTED READING ACTIVITY

NON–FICTION SHORTCUTS

FAST-TRACKING COMPREHENSION

BEFORE

1. KWLW (First 2 parts; Know, Want To Know)

2. Super Skim; Slow Skim

3. PWR—(Predict, Write)

4. Write Questions (Turn 'Heads' into Questions)

5. Book Walk (Chapter Walk):
   - Notice author's pattern (main ideas)
   - Notice pictures, photos, charts
   - Notice heads/captions
   - Notice sections/themes
   - Look for signal words and phrases
   - Read, write down questions at end of chapter or section
   - Read summary at end
   - Read 1st & last paragraph of chapter or section
   - Write down important or new vocabulary words

DURING

1. RCRC (Read, Cover or Close, Recite or Retell, Check)

2. Vocabulary (Web) or other strategies.

AFTER

1. Check Predictions

2. Answer your initial questions

3. Re-Skim; Dip into areas you were unsure of

4. Vocabulary Review

5. KWLW (Last 2 parts—Learned; Want To Know)

6. RCRC (Last 2 parts)

Thoughts and Ideas

144

KWLW WALL CHART

K	W	L	W
I Know	I Want To Know	I Learned	I Want To Know

KWLW wall chart, smart board or student worksheet.

*KWLW adapted by Rita Wirtz from Ogle's original KWL format.

KWLWW WALL CHART

K	W	L	W	W
I Know	I Want To Know	I Learned	I Want To Know	Where I'll Find It

KWLWW wall chart, smart board or student worksheet.

*KWLWW adapted by Rita Wirtz from Ogle's original KWL format.

TEACHING TERRIFIC TEXTBOOKS

Book Walk—Pre-Reading Skills

1. Read the front and back of the book.
2. Read the foreword and introduction.
3. Read the table of contents—the author's outline.
4. Look at any charts, diagrams, pictures, glossary, index, etc.
5. Notice any special features. Skim the book for format.
6. Skim the entire book at one page per second, up to a minute.
7. Look for key ideas. 'Web' the book.
8. Use mindmapping or other graphic organizers to outline the book.
9. First and last chapter—introduce, and summarize content.
10. First and last paragraph in chapter—introduce and summarize content.
11. Look for topic and summary sentences throughout.
12. Find Author's Pattern. (See accompanying explanation.)
13. Note that <u>verbs</u> and <u>nouns</u> of a sentence offer the most important information. (Berg)
14. Watch for negative words like *not, no, can't*—may reverse meaning. (Berg)
15. Teach signposts and signals which add to meaning:

A. *Qualifying words—however, moreover, nevertheless*, change entire meaning.
B. *Enumerative words—first, next,* tell the reader the sequence.
C. *Contrast words—yet, nevertheless, otherwise, although, despite, in spite of, not, or, nor, however, on the contrary,* change the thought.
D. *Go ahead words—such as, and, more than that, more, moreover, likewise.*
E. *Time Signals—before, since, earlier, to begin with, after, later, next, soon, finally, last.*
F. *Connectives— if, so, finally, therefore, eventhough, however, so on.*

16. Teach students to skim, scan, and find main or big ideas.
17. When Book Walking a text chapter, double skim, more slowly the second time.
18. Make predictions about what the book (or a specific chapter) will be about.

To get results, *spend 60% time previewing,* 30% reading *and 10% of the time* reviewing. ***Emphasis on note taking and studying.***

EASY START TEXT WEB

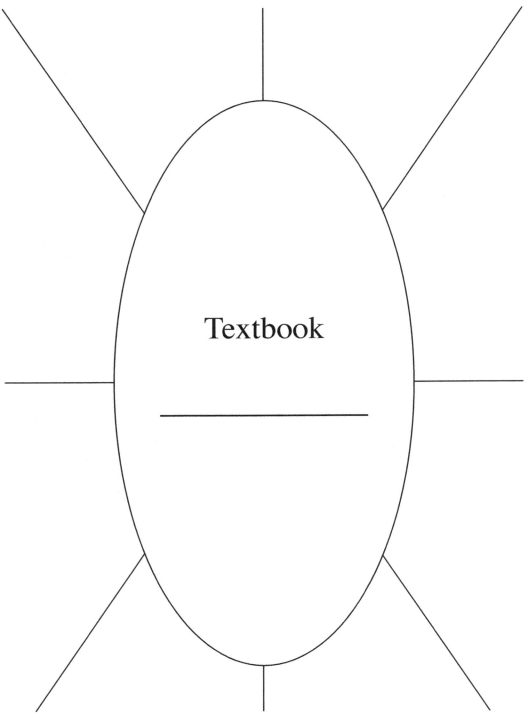

Textbook

Web the chapters or sections of the textbook, before you start reading, for the 'global' or big picture.

TEXT PRACTICE

Tell students to open their textbook to the beginning of a given chapter. Allow five or so minutes to preview the title, formulate a purpose or purposes for reading, and grasp at least two main ideas so they will be able to write a brief outline or summary. Ask them to close their books and then write the title, purposes for reading, and brief outline or summary. Optional, do partner sharing.

Repeat this with your students often, so they get in the habit of doing this excellent study technique.

---

1. *Chapter title* _____
2. *Title means* _____

_____

3. *Purpose for reading* _____

_____

_____

_____

_____

_____

4. *Big ideas* _____

_____

_____

_____

_____

_____

_____

_____

_____

_____

_____

_____

WHAT IT'S ABOUT: FOUR BIG IDEAS

Use as a wall chart or other. Read to find out big ideas *Before, During, After* reading. *Sequence* may be recorded with this format.

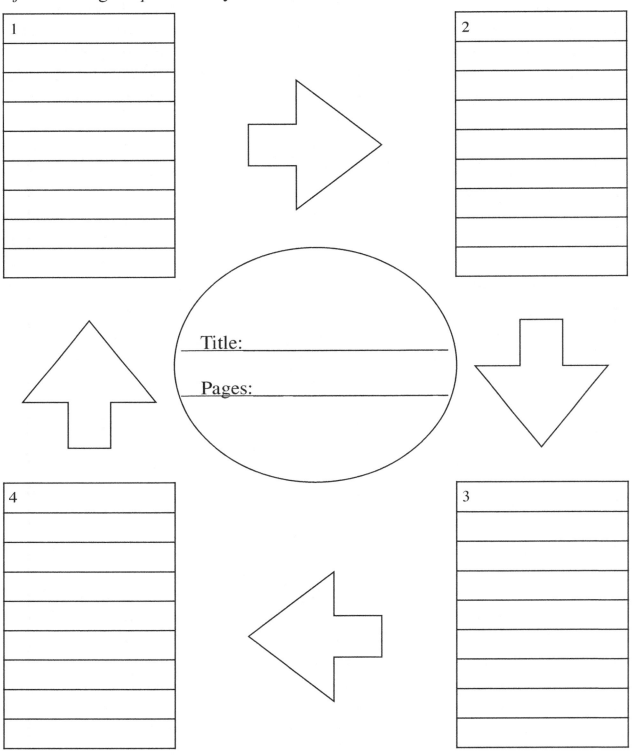

QUESTION/PAGE/ANSWER READING FOR INFORMATION

Things to look for while you read. Read to find out

Question		Answer
	Page	
	Page	
	Page	
	Page	
	Page	

Various uses of this strategy

Variation .1: List questions you want students to read to find out, and page numbers. At designated time, students provide answers they found.

Variation 2: Students skim through the chapter writing questions and corresponding page numbers (worksheets or scratch paper). *Boardwork*. At designated time, start with one student, as a model. He/she calls out a question and page; class skims for answer. First correct goes next with a question. Great pre-reading activities.

Variation 3: As a *During Reading* activity, students continue to write answers as they read.

READING CHAMPIONSHIP
STRATEGY 1—PWR

1	P	**Predict** *Guess what the paragraph, page, or chapter is about*
2	W	**Write** *Write down your guess about the information*
3	R	**Read** *Read to find out if you were right*

Now, go back to step one and read another part

STRATEGY 2—RCRC

1	R	**Read It** *Read the information.*
2	C	**Cover It** *Cover up what you read, or close the book.*
3	R	**Recite It** *Say what you just read to yourself or to someone else.*
4	C	**Check It** *Open the book and quickly reread to see if you are right.*

Now, go back to step one and read another part

STRATEGY 3—PWRCRC

1	P	**Predict** *Guess what the paragraph, page, or chapter is about.*
2	W	**Write** *Write down your guess about the information.*
3	R	**Read** *Read to find out if you were right.*
4	C	**Cover** *Cover the page or close the book.*
5	R	**Recite/Retell** *Say what you just read out loud to yourself or tell someone else.*
6	C	**Check** *Open the book and skim that part again — (Did you understand and remember what you read?).*

Now, go back to step one and read another part

BASIC BLOOM'S TAXONOMY

Level	What	Do
KNOWLEDGE	State the basic facts	Name, List, Tell, Define, Describe
COMPREHENSION	Understand the concept	Discuss, Summarize, Explain, Demonstrate, Review
APPLICATION	Use the information	Show, Apply, Produce, Draw, Select
ANALYSIS	Check the parts	Compare, Contrast, Debate, Classify, Diagram
SYNTHESIS	Put information together	Design, Create, Construct, Perform, Organize
EVALUATION	Form an opinion	Decide, Conclude, Rank, Rate, Prove

(Based on Bloom's Taxonomy). Enlarge to wall chart, reproduce for students' notebooks. Use this thinking process with students, skill levels 2-Adult.

EASY START Q & A

BEFORE & AFTER READING

Q	A
(Questions) Before	(Answer) After

Use as wall chart, or other. Brainstorm questions with group. Read. Record answers, after reading. Review with class.

QUESTIONS, ANSWERS, DETAILS

Q, A & D

1 QUESTIONS (BEFORE)	2 ANSWERS (AFTER)	3 IMPORTANT DETAIL	4 PAGE NUMBER

Enlarge to wall chart, (laminate), smart board or other. Alone, partners, whole group.

COMPREHENSION QAR
Easy Start Finding Answers to Questions.

1. It's right there. Read carefully. The answer is usually the same words in the question.	**Literal**
2. Look for it. The answer isn't there directly, but put the pieces of information together.	**Interpretive**
3. Use your experience. Use what you know already to figure it out.	**Application**

Adapted from QAR (Question—Answer Relationships) by Raphael, 1984. Model this strategy often, using informational or narrative text. Practice paragraph by paragraph in given text. Use this format as wall chart, on smart board or photocopy for students' notebooks.

AUTHOR'S PATTERN
TEXT STRATEGY

This is an excellent strategy to use with your class. Teach them how to determine the pattern of the author's writing style. This helps locate the main ideas and supporting details. Select 2-3 paragraphs from different chapters of the book, and determine how the author has written the book. This technique increases comprehension.

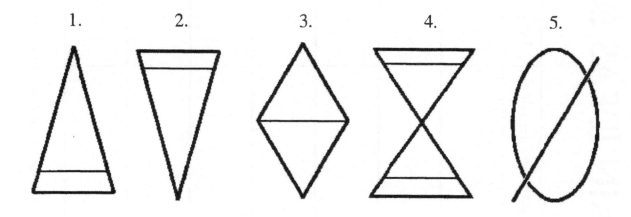

1.   Main idea is at the bottom of the paragraph. Details lead up to the main idea at the end.

2.   Main idea is at the beginning, usually the first sentence of the paragraph. Details follow.

3.   Main idea is in the middle of the paragraph. Details start and end the section.

4.   Main idea is at the beginning of the paragraph and at the end. Details are in the middle.

5.   Ambiguous or inconsistent pattern. Poor writing style for a reader to follow. Use another strategy. (Two or more authors.)

Concept originators Silvaroli and Edwards, Adapted by Rita Wirtz.

EASY START—MAIN IDEAS & DETAILS

Page	Write the main idea	Draw the main idea	Write a detail	Draw a detail
1				
2				
3				
4				
5				
6				
7				

Use as student worksheet, or enlarge to poster size (laminate). Model with informational text. Do paragraph by paragraph to start. Alone or with a partner. Share out loud with whole class.

THE SIX W'S OF COMPREHENSION

QUESTION	ANSWER
WHO	
WHAT	
WHEN	
WHERE	
HOW	
WHY	

Use as wall chart, or student worksheet. Or enlarge to poster size (laminate). Practice out loud after each informational text piece. Say "Who was it about?" (class answers in choral response) etc. down the list, as base review *or* have partners ask (quiz) each other.

EASY START HERRINGBONE

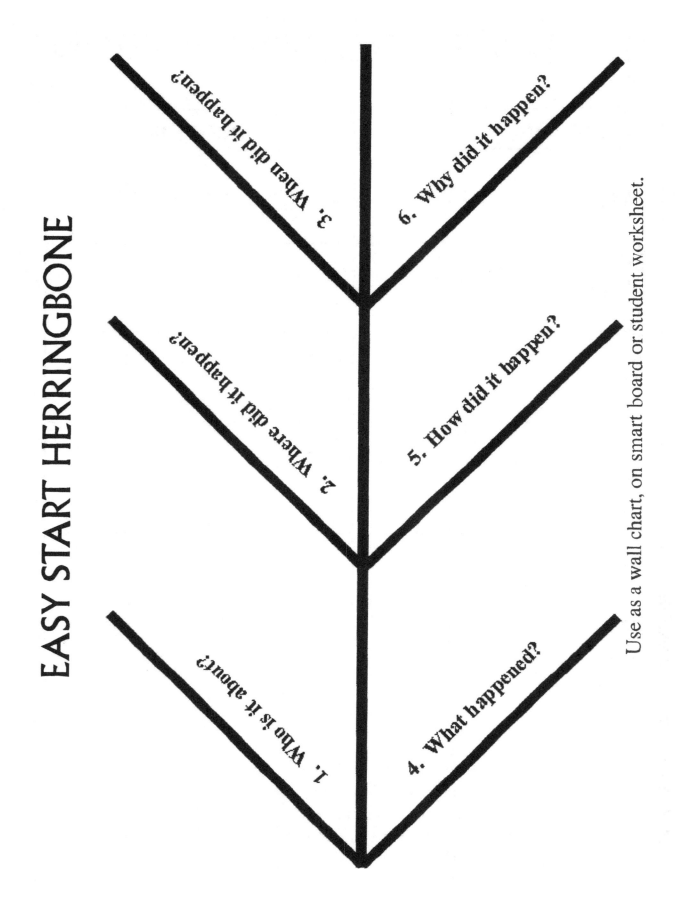

3. When did it happen?

6. Why did it happen?

2. Where did it happen?

5. How did it happen?

1. Who is it about?

4. What happened?

Use as a wall chart, on smart board or student worksheet.

EASY START RESPONSE JOURNAL
WHAT IT'S ABOUT

Write what it's about in 20 words or less. (10 words, 5 words, or less). Use with smart board or reproducible student worksheet. Or enlarge to poster size wall chart (laminate). Do as individual, small group, or whole class instruction.

1. **Paragraph 1**

   _____
   _____
   _____
   _____
   _____
   _____

2. **Paragraph 2**

   _____
   _____
   _____
   _____
   _____
   _____

3. **Paragraph 3**

   _____
   _____
   _____
   _____

4. **Paragraph 4**

   _____
   _____
   _____
   _____
   _____
   _____

5. **Paragraph 5**

   _____
   _____
   _____
   _____
   _____
   _____

6. **Paragraph 6**

   _____
   _____
   _____
   _____

EASY START NOTES

Main idea (Draw it)   **Main idea (Write it)**

1 _____ Page
2 _____
3 _____
4 _____

1 _____ Page
2 _____
3 _____
4 _____

1 _____ Page
2 _____
3 _____
4 _____

1 _____ Page
2 _____
3 _____
4 _____

Do by page or paragraph. Use as student reproducible worksheet. Or enlarge to poster size wall chart (laminate). Do individually, or pairs.

MORE TIPS FOR BOOSTING COMPREHENSION—NON-FICTION

Tony Buzan, in *Speed Reading,* says knowing how paragraphs are organized helps increase speed and comprehension.

He describes paragraphs as *explanatory, descriptive,* or *linking.* In explanatory look for the topic sentence or main idea to be near the top of the paragraph, with details in the middle, and the conclusion somewhere near the end.

Descriptive paragraphs have lots of details, few big main ideas. Linking paragraphs according to Buzan, have important information and do lots of summarizing.

Howard Stephen Berg, in *Super Reading Secrets,* suggests three steps: first, skim, at two to five seconds per page. This is the time to check out the things which stand out, any special textual features. Next, have a purpose and read actively. Finally, study material, retaining as much information as possible.

In *Breakthrough Rapid Reading,* Peter Kump suggests that there are five levels of information to look for in reading: the book's main idea, main point of each chapter, main point of each section within chapters, main point of most paragraphs, details within each paragraph.

FINAL COMMENTS: CHAPTER 7

NON-FICTION: TEACH YOUR STUDENTS

1. Notice how the material is organized. Some typical patterns include:
   - cause and effect
   - chronological order
   - spatial
   - comparison and contrast
   - relevance (how important?)
2. Use your index finger to move your eyes along lines of print.
3. Have a purpose for your reading, every time.
4. The more prior knowledge regarding a subject, the faster you read.
5. Read more then one word at a time; read phrases, lines, sections, words around words (paragraphs), etc.
6. Read silently without saying words to yourself. This is called sub-vocalizing; fast reading is silent reading.
7. Signal and transition words help you shift gears in your reading. Watch for *before, then, next, more, however,* etc.
8. To *skim,* read quickly down the lines of print. In *Breakthrough Rapid Reading,* Peter Kump suggests the best way is to "read the first paragraph or two, then read topic sentences of all the paragraphs as quickly as you can." He suggests you use an underlining hand movement.
9. To *scan,* look for specific information on a page. This is not the same as skimming, although many people think these are the same thing.
10. Read a speed reading book, and practice the exercises, daily Or take a reading class at your local Jr. College, or University. Many community services, such as Parks and Recreation, offer free or low cost courses.

Chapter 8
Easy Start Memory Joggers

*To remember, the learning
must be memorable.
"Repetition makes the learning stick."*

Rita Wirtz

Recent advances in brain research help learning diverse students master fundamental standards- based reading skills. In order to meet special needs of all students, including second language learners, special education and Title 1 students it is imperative to review how memory processes work. The importance of brain-compatible classroom strategies which assist in comprehending written materials, remembering and recalling information cannot be overstated.

This unique chapter summarizes and specifies the best of what is currently known about the learning cycle, study skills and tips which improve memory and classroom strategies which help ensure mastery of all standards- based lessons from word recognition through literary and textual analysis.

*Memory Joggers
Keys to Comprehension Success
Best Comprehension/Memory Techniques
Easy Start Study Tips
Teach Skills; Model Attitudes*

INTRODUCTION TO CHAPTER 8

EASY START MEMORY JOGGERS

1. Have a reason to know it.
2. Chunk it into pieces.
3. Practice it frequently.
4. Repeat it (practice).
5. Overlearn it (repetition).
6. Breathe deeply to de-stress.
7. Drink water (lots).
8. Take breaks often.
9. Vary your 'place' (of study).
10. Play Baroque music.*
11. Add emotion to motivate.
12. Use color to stimulate.
13. Use scent (such as cinnamon).
14. Add novelty to stand out.
15. Exaggerate it.
16. Write what you've learned.
17. Tell someone else.
18. Make a model.

---

*Best of Baroque: play only 10-20 minutes of each hour. Calms students, and aids memory.

Pachelbel's *Canon*; Vivaldi's *4 Seasons*; Handel's *Water Music*; Corelli's *Pastorale*; Bach's *Air for the G-String*; Albinoni's *Adagio,* Bach's *Brandenburg Concertos.* Any *Best of* Baroque .

KEYS TO
COMPREHENSION SUCCESS

Key Points

The two best tools for improving memory and recall are *repetition* (rote learning) and *association/ connection* (linkages). Add in *emotion* and *involvement* and there is a better chance students remember what they have learned or read.

Memory patterning in the brain begins with sensory memory—a one or two second memory attached to stimuli. If the brain thinks something is important and 'attends to it', it moves into short-term memory which lasts about twenty seconds. Long-term memory needs *meaning* and *emotion*.

The learning cycle consists of:

1. Interest, or attention.

2. Information.

3. Processing.

4. Conclusion.

5. Application/transfer.

Memory researchers tell us that the space in short-term memory is between five and seven bits of information. This is called 'M' space of memory capacity. It is less for young children and increases with age. So, teach in *chunks*. Chunk everything with a *Set* and *Close* in each chunk.

NOTES:

SOME OF THE BEST COMPREHENSION/ MEMORY TECHNIQUES

1. Teach students how to remember lists by *chunking*, or separating into smaller groups (examples— phone numbers). *Downchunking* is breaking up material into smaller units. *Upchunking* means seeing the bigger picture.

2. Use stories, metaphors, proverbs and analogies for emotional association.

3. Use Peg Mnemonics: Come up with new images to go with the numbers one—ten. Use rhyming objects like one–ton, two–shoe, three–tree (read Tony Buzan's memory books). Ostrander and Schroeder suggest numbering on the family's hierarchy or using body parts, such as one-head, etc.

4. Teach the global first, analytic parts, then back to the global.

5. Use the concept of *overlearning* for rote work. Overlearning is *repetition*.

6. Process all new material in an active rather than passive way.

7. Model the learning.

8. Use the Von Restorff Effect— humorous, colorful and most unusual things are easily remembered. These special effects make words, ideas, and objects stand out from the rest (example—butter, table, fort, picture, mother, couch, Tarzan The Ape Man).

9. Hang visuals at eye level (as students are seated).

10. Hermann Ebbinghaus, a German memory researcher gave us the *Ebbinghaus curve of forgetting*. Subsequent researchers conclude that the ideal practice or mental review should occur within eight to twelve seconds, thirty to fifty seconds, five to ten minutes later, one day, one week, one month, four months.

11. Use Baroque as a background music booster. Its special beat tunes students' brains into excellent concentration. Matches heartbeat—60-80 beats per minute (Jensen).

12. Use memory association. Tony Buzan suggests creating colorful, moving, three-dimensional mental images. Add in the sound, sight and smell of things to make the association with the learning. Use all modalities and the senses. This is called *Synesthesia* (Immersion)!

13. Another mnemonic device is called *location*. To remember a list of unrelated items, associate each item with a part of a house.

14. Use strong Sets and Closes, connecting with students' *Schema* (prior knowledge). (For more information, see enclosed)

15. Teach according to **Primacy** and **Recency**. Remember, students remember best the first part of the lesson, unit, or the day; last part comes next, with middle nearly forgotten, unless elaborate rehearsal strategies are used. Teach in *chunks*. (For more information, see enclosed.)

16. Use rhythm to structure material students need to memorize.

Lofland suggests teaching in *lexical units*. To do this, speak for four seconds, pause for four seconds. Each is a short lexical unit. Use this material for spelling words, historical dates, and math problems. Your information must be a chunk of five to nine pieces.

17. Act it Out.

18. Create a scene. Pantomime the scene from the textbook or story.

19. Use graphic organizers such as Web, Matrix (Grid), Venn Diagram, Story Boards, etc. (enclosed)

20. Strategies including SQ3R, (Survey, Question, Read, Recite, Review) SPD (Survey, Predict, Decide) and RCRC (Read, Cover or Close, Retell or Recite, Check).

21. Games!

22. KWLW – Charts, or on paper put K is what I know, W is what I want to know, L is what I learned after-ward, and W is for want to know more. For the columns, K is on the left third, W in the middle, L and W are on the right hand columns. (For more information, see enclosed).

23. Wisdom Storm! Brainstorm what is known about the topic first.

24. Wall Chart – Place a poster with the main idea of the reading material. Working alone or in groups, write one main idea per sign – students cover a wall or bulletin board with the story ideas. Teacher can also do a 'starter' for sequencing.

25. Author's Pattern – Use Author's Pattern with your students to find main ideas (enclosed).

26. Bloom's Taxonomy. (See Basic Bloom's Taxonomy (enclosed).

27. WAIT TIME – Vary your responses; do more clarifying.

28. Summarize what has just been read. Think—Pair—Share partner sharing. Think, then tell a learning partner. (Think, Ink, and Speak variation—Think, Write, say out loud, or tell a partner).

29. Request: on one-to-one, students ask teacher or other students questions about what has been read, by line, paragraph, or page.

30. Plays, choral reading, reader's theatre, poems, and puppetry. Have fun!

31. Write about the reading (journal, or log).

32. Create a rap or a song about the reading. Write a Haiku or other poem.

33. Draw what you read. Do a story map (enclosed).

34. Use props to stimulate interest. (Stuff from home.)

35. Your success secrets:

"Practice Makes Permanent." Practice Daily.

---

* Robert Sylwester, a Professor at the University of Oregon.

EASY START STUDY TIPS

1. See it—Read page or chapter.
   Say it—Recite out loud, or to a friend.
   Close it—Close the book.
   Repeat it—Say out loud.
   Practice it—Different ways.
2. Set a timer for each subject's study time.
3. Keep your place as you read. Use your finger or bookmark.
4. Concentrate. Do one thing at a time.
5. Study every day in short blocks.
6. Drink lots of water. Avoid caffeine.
7. Mix carbohydrates with protein, to stay alert.
8. Study different subjects in different rooms or parts of a room.
9. Color code; use sticky notes on book pages.
10. Use study notes, formats, and graphic organizers.

FINAL COMMENTS: CHAPTER 8

1. Teach skills. Model attitudes.

2. Model everything, at least three times, in three ways.

3. Drill. Lots of *repetition, practice*, and *review*.

4. Repertoire
   3 R's: <u>R</u>isk + <u>R</u>epertoire = <u>R</u>esults!

5. *Improve reading by:*
   - A.   Need to know.
   - B.   Interest to learn.
   - C.   Motivation to practice.
   - D.   Lots of reading variety.

Chapter 9
How Reading Champions Read Fiction

Motivate Kids to Read and Teach Basic Skills

This chapter assists teachers plan and instruct strategies matching standards in literary response and analysis. "Students read and respond to a wide variety of significant works of children's literature. They distinguish between the structural features of text and literary terms or elements (e.g., theme, plot, setting, characters." (State Standards). Story structure maps and other tools help students build an appreciation for and understanding of people, places, events and conflicts which occur in literary models and genres.

Many of the same comprehension considerations taught in the last chapter, teaching non-fiction are readily transferred to narrative text. ***Reading Champions!*** strategies supplement many standards-based lessons in literary analysis and response, including such skills as predictions, setting, plot, characters, theme, point of view, tone or mood, conflict, cause and effect, foreshadowing, irony, figurative language etc.

Teach Core Literature Classics
Favorite Core Literature
Theme Read-O-Rama
Book Reports, Reading Record
Literature Book Walk
Making Predictions
Summarizing and Sequence Organizers
Story Grammar Map
Setting, Plot Charts and Character Web
Motivating Students to Read Fiction

INTRODUCTION TO CHAPTER 9
TEACH CORE LITERATURE CLASSICS

Accelerate the basics. Goal is class study of one novel per month. Here are the basic elements to include:

1. *SET/CLOSE:* 'Open' & 'Close' the book as a whole, & each section.

2. *PREDICTIONS:* Guess what it's about; what's happening next?

3. *BOOK WALK:* General idea of novel.

4. *SETTING:* When & Where? Descriptions.

5. *PLOT:*
   A. (Beginning, Middle, End) The events of the story. What's happening?
   B. Story Grammar (enclosed).

6. *CHARACTERS:* Who; What they say, do; others' reaction to them.

7. *TONE/MOOD:* How does it feel?

8. *THEME:* What is the 'message'? What's it about?

9. *POINT OF VIEW:* Who's telling the story?

10. *CONFLICT:* Events/Problems/Solutions. (Against self, nature, others).

11. *CAUSE & EFFECT:* If 'this' happens, then 'this' happens.

12. *COMPARE & CONTRAST:* (Same or different).

13. *SEQUENCE:* The order of things.

14. *VOCABULARY:* Find new, interesting, important to know, or fun-to-say words.

15. *DECODING:* Phonics Review, especially structural analysis.

16. *FIGURATIVE LANGUAGE:* Metaphors, Similes, Personification.

17. *IRONY:* Something different than expected.

18. *FORESHADOWING:* What's coming next?

19. *COMPRHENSION:* Finding the meaning. Understanding what you read.

20. *GENRE:* Type of book—biography, historical fiction, science fiction, etc.

FAVORITE CORE LITERATURE CLASSICS

(Skill Levels 3–9)

James and the Giant Peach (Dahl)

Charlotte's Web (E.B. White)

Sarah Plain and Tall (MacLachlan)

Stone Fox (Gardiner)

Indian in the Cupboard (Banks)

Castle in the Attic (Winthrop)

Island of the Blue Dolphins (O'Dell)

Dear Mr. Henshaw (Cleary)

Matilda (Dahl)

A Wrinkle in Time (L'Engle)

Tuck Everlasting (Babbitt)

Bridge to Terabithia (Paterson)

The Giver (Lowry)

Hatchet & The River (Paulsen)

Sign of the Beaver (Speare)

I Heard the Owl Call My Name (Craven)

Courage of Sarah Noble (Dalgliesh)

Children of the River (Crew)

Yolanda's Genius (Fenner)

Dragonwings (Yep)

The House on Mango Street (Cisneros)

Roll of Thunder, Hear My Cry (Taylor)

The Cay (Taylor)

Old Man and the Sea (Hemingway)

Call of The Wild (London)

Call it Courage (Sperry)

Witch of Blackbird Pond (Speare)

My Brother Sam Is Dead (Collier & Collier)

Patty Reed's Doll; Story of the Donner Party (Laurgaard)

By the Great Horn Spoon (Fleischman)

The Diary of A Young Girl (Anne Frank)

Summer of the Monkeys & Where the Red Fern Grows (Rawls)

Sarah Bishop (O'Dell)

Harriet The Spy (Fitzhugh)

The Phantom Tollbooth (Juster)

Caddie Woodlawn (Brink)

Number The Stars (Lowry)

The Lion, The Witch, and The Wardrobe (Lewis)

THEME READ-O-RAMA

There are 12 themes which match the novel a month goal. Read a novel with a different theme, each month. At a minimum, make sure students read novels with these themes throughout the year. To teach *theme*, students must make inferences about their reading, drawing on personal experience.

12 Most Frequent Themes in Core (Classic) Literature

1. Love
2. Friendship
3. Friends
4. Family
5. Loyalty
6. Courage
7. Conflicts
8. Heroes & Sheroes (Heroines)
9. Adventure
10. Making tough decisions
11. Enemy to friend
12. Dying

Easy Start Goal

1. Provide examples from the novel which supports the theme.
2. Write about the theme.

ONE MINUTE BOOK REPORT

Do out loud, whole class, in partners, or written. All skill levels, part or all of the class, daily.

1. Book Title _____

_____

2. Why you should read this book: _____

_____

_____

_____

_____

_____

_____

1. Book Title _____

_____

2. Why you should read this book: _____

_____

_____

_____

_____

_____

_____

1. Book Title _____

_____

2. Why you should read this book: _____

_____

_____

_____

_____

_____

1. Book Title _____

_____

2. Why you should read this book: _____

_____

_____

_____

_____

_____

WHY I LOVE THIS BOOK

I love this book _____(title).

I couldn't put this book down because:

_____

_____

_____

My favorite character is:

_____

_____

My favorite part is:

_____

_____

You should read this book because:_____

_____

_____

Next I'm going to read:

_____

_____

All skill levels:
1. Do out loud, taking turns.
2. *Or* do as (oral) partner share.
3. Anchor chart, smart board, or
    worksheet to turn in.

WHAT I THINK ABOUT WHAT I READ

Do out loud, in partners, or written. Time this.

1. This is what I read:

(title) _____

_____

_____

2. What it was all about:

_____

_____

_____

_____

3. This is what I think about

what I read: _____

_____

_____

_____

4. Why I (would or wouldn't)

recommend reading this:

_____

_____

_____

_____

_____

5. Next I'm going to read:

_____

_____

_____

_____

_____

TALK ABOUT WHAT YOU'VE READ

(Skill levels 3–Adult)

Number off into partners (1's & 2's).

Partner #1 has one minute (3, 5 minutes) to describe as many of these elements as possible from current novel study:
characters, setting, sequence, point of view, story grammar, etc.

Partner #2 shares areas of agreement and disagreement. After designated time is up, taking turns, partners state "One thing I learned is ..."

Both students turn in to teacher on scratch paper, "One thing I learned:" Fun activity, class and teacher teach and assess simultaneously.

Core Literature

Name _____

Date _____

Book _____

One Thing That I Learned: _____

_____

_____

WHAT I READ THIS WEEK

(Skill levels 3–Adult)

This is fun to do at the end of each week (Works well at home or school...)

Say out loud

"You have 1 (2 or 3) minute(s) to list as many kinds (and titles) of books, magazines, articles, newspapers, and text books you read this week". Time it. It might be fun to chart it as a form of assessment/progress chart. Do as a report to teacher, or students in pairs or small groups (or whole class).

Write it down:

Time this exercise. Say "You have (2 or 3) minute(s) to write as many kinds (and titles) of books, magazines, articles, newspapers, and text books you read this week". Exchange papers in a round.

What I Read This Week Chart

> A. What I read this week. I read...
>
> (or)
>
> B. What I read this week and what it was about...
>
> (or)
>
> C. What I read this week and who wrote it.
>
> (or)
>
> D. What I read this week and did I like it? Why or why not?

READING RECORD
(Skill levels 3-Adult)

Goals:
1. Read every day.
2. Read more pages each day.
3. Spend more time reading each day.
4. Read for pleasure and information.

Name_____ **Week Of:**_____

1. This Week 1'11 Read:

Novel(s) _____

Magazine(s) _____

Textbook(s) _____

Newspaper(s) _____

Internet _____

Other _____

2. How I Did.

I Read: _____

Library Visits (bonus):_____

A NOVEL IDEA—FICTION
CORE LITERATURE BOOK WALK

1. Read the title of the novel, out loud.

2. Look at the pictures on the front and back cover, if any. Do the pictures hint (*foreshadow*) the setting, time, characters? Read the back cover.

3. Make *predictions* about what the whole novel may be about. Write questions to read to find out.

4. Are the chapters numbered and named? If so, web the titles and make predictions about what these might be about.

5. Who is the author? Do you know about this author already? Have you read any other books by this author? Read any available information about the author.

6. When was this book written? Is the date important to this story?

7. Read the Foreword or Introduction.

8. *Genre*—what type of book is this? Have you read anything else in this genre? (historical fiction, biography, science fiction, etc.)

9. Open the book to the first chapter. Read only the first paragraph to feel the tone or style of the book, and see what information you get.

10. Glance through the sections of the book, especially noting any photos, illustrations, or other information that stands out.

11. Note any specialized vocabulary.

12. Do a KWLW about book's topic (enclosed).

Use as whole class process, smart board or wall chart (enlarge to poster size (laminate). Or photocopy for students' notebooks, as an instant reference.

EASY START LITERATURE REVIEW

1. Prediction(s)	2. Setting	3. Plot
4. Characters	5. Sequence	6. Tone/Mood 7. Irony
8. Theme	9. Point of View	10. Figurative Language

Use as wall chart, on smart board (oral work), or student worksheet. These are the most basic elements to include in *narrative text*, core literature study.

THINK & FEEL ABOUT IT

Pre-reading activity. Use with whole class, (orally) or student worksheet. Or enlarge to poster size class chart (laminate).

Idea or statement	Before Reading	After Reading
1.		
2.		
3.		
4.		
5.		
6.		

I THINK THAT

MAKING PREDICTIONS

1. GUESS WHAT IT'S ABOUT

I think that it's about

_____

_____
_____
_____
_____

2. READ IT

I was right

_____
_____
_____

I was not right

_____
_____

_____
_____
_____

I was sort of right

_____
_____
_____

3. GUESS AGAIN

I think that

_____
_____
_____
_____
_____
_____

4. READ AGAIN

Keep repeating until you've read it all. How are your _predictions_ today?

Name: _____

Date: _____

Title: _____

Look/Guess/Decide Prediction Strategy

1. Think what might happen next.
2. Take a guess. Write it down, or tell your reading partner.
3. Decide if you were right by reading the next sentence or paragraph.

GUESS What I think will happen	PAGE	WHAT HAPPENED The author wrote

4. Continue on with the reading.

EASY START SUMMARIZING

Combine with Retellings, out loud with a partner

Students *summarize* each part of the book, chapter, page or paragraph. Fold construction or other plain paper into an *Eight Box Fold* which can be used front and back (16 short summaries), or use this format. (Write, and/or draw.)

1.	2.
3.	4.
5.	6.
7.	8.

EASY START STORY GRAMMAR MAP

1. WHO	2. WHERE	3. WHEN

4. WHAT	5. FIX IT

1. WHO are the main characters?
2. WHERE does the story take place?
3. WHEN does the story take place?
4. WHAT is the problem? (Oops!)
5. FIX IT- How do the characters solve the problem?

*Use with each chapter, or whole book or story. Wall chart, smart board or worksheet Students draw and write in each box. With variations, skill levels K-Adult.

WHERE IT TAKES PLACE

EASY START SETTING PRACTICE

(Skill Levels 3–Adult)

BEFORE READING

As far as you have previewed, or read, describe the setting.

1. Say it	**2. Write it**	**3. Draw it**

DURING READING

1. Has the setting for the novel changed (describe how) or remained unchanged?

2. When does the novel take place (day? season? month? and year?).

AFTER READING

1. Was the setting the same throughout the novel?

2. Describe each of the settings.

THINK ABOUT IT

1. How does the setting contribute to the novel?

2. Would the novel be different in a different setting?

EASY START PLOT CHART #1

THIS BOOK'S ABOUT

Chapter, Book or Story	1. Beginning The plot begins with:	2. Middle The middle part is about:	3. End This happens at the end:

*Use with each chapter, or whole book or story. Skill Levels 1-Adult. Smart board or enlarge to poster size classroom wall chart.

EASY START PLOT CHART #2

BME—What It's About

(Skill levels 1–Adult)

1. Beginning What it's about	2. Middle What it's about	3. End What it's about

Use as a wall chart, smart board or worksheet. A solid, quick chart. BME Chart can also be used as a three box fold.

EASY START CHARACTER WEB

Book

_____

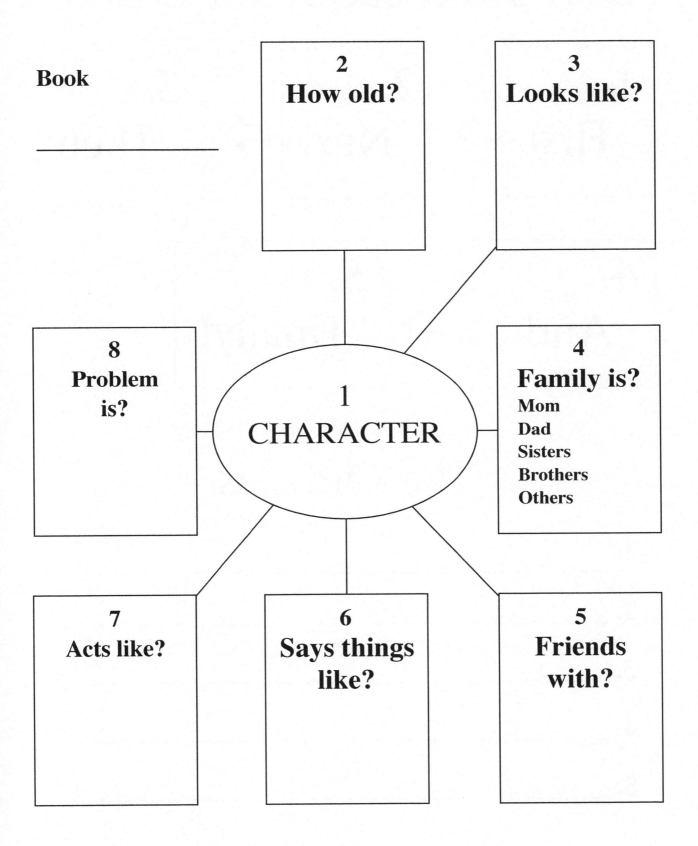

2
How old?

3
Looks like?

8
**Problem
is?**

1
CHARACTER

4
Family is?
Mom
Dad
Sisters
Brothers
Others

7
Acts like?

6
**Says things
like?**

5
**Friends
with?**

EASY START SEQUENCE CHART

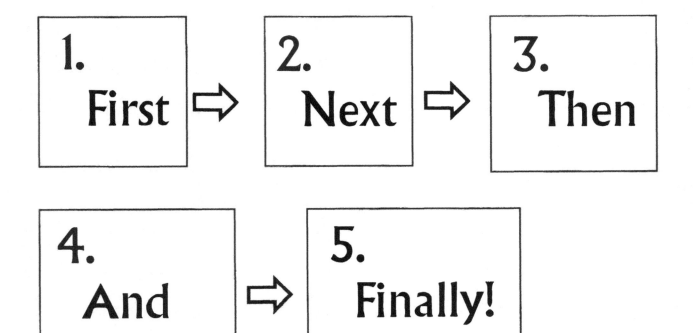

The Order is

1. _____

2. _____

3. _____

4. _____

5. _____

EASY START STORYBOARD SEQUENCE

Use the accompanying storyboard format. Enlarge into chart size (laminated to write on). As whole class or small group activity, sequence the order of the story. Great smart board whole class activity, or reproduce as student worksheets.

Here's What Happened		
First	Next ⇨	Next ⇨
Then	Then ⇨	Finally

STORYBOARD SEQUENCE FORMAT

EASY START COMPARE & CONTRAST
VENN DIAGRAM

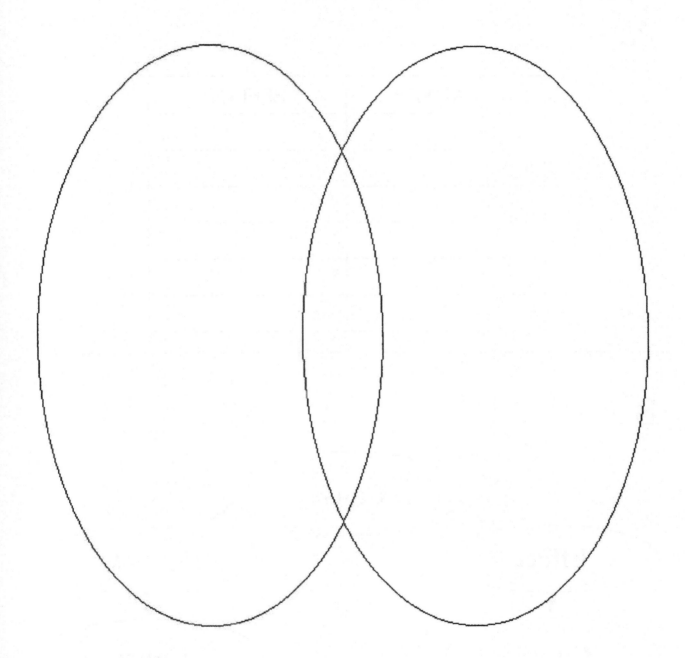

With variation, skill levels K-Adult.
Use a Venn Diagram to compare/contrast two characters, places, or things.
Do on smart board , enlarge to poster size wall chart (laminate) or duplicate for
student worksheets.

EASY START CAUSE & EFFECT

Here are two easy to-do maps. Use as wall chart, overhead, or student worksheet.

A.

CAUSE	EFFECT
1	1
2	2
3	3
4	4
5	5
6	6

B.

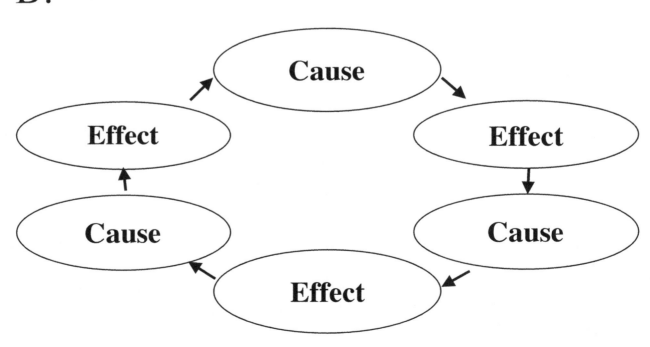

FINAL COMMENTS: CHAPTER 9
MOTIVATE STUDENTS TO READ FICTION!

To motivate students to read fiction, *you've got to read.*

Tell them about

    a.) Why you chose what you read and what you've learned from it.

    b.) Whether you like what you've read.

    c.) What you are reading next and why.

Keep up a continual dialogue about what everyone's reading. Be exciting and motivating about reading, and learning to read better.

It's always a good idea to chart reading done individually, or as a group, or class. Chart by titles read by total class; individual students keep their own charts.

In the 70's, Dr. Harry Singer, of University of California Riverside wrote about the value of charting as a motivator and an easy way to track skills mastered, in any area. This still stands up. So chart as much as you can, as often as you can, to show growth, and books read.

MOTIVATING STUDENTS TO READ FICTION, YOUR THINKING:

ADDENDUM

P.S.

Want to Learn ONE More Thing?

Selected Resources
…To continue your study …

FUN STUFF TO DO—
OVER & OVER

1. Make Phonics Origami (folds, throughout this book).

2. Use Manipulatives—word and letter tiles.

3. Use Fun Framers to frame words, parts of speech,
    phonics element, index card, bookmark, word wand
    (half pipe cleaner, end formed in an oval).

4. Make pop-up books for vocabulary words, comprehension strategy,
    phonics element, etc.

5. Make Flip Books. Use with magic markers, if possible. Use for skill
    drills (whole class) and partner practice.

6. Use rubber band books, mini books *all* the time. (Have students
    create five to six sets at once; teacher keeps and distributes when
    ready.)

7. Go to your local copy center. Make color transparencies (enlarge to 8
    1/2 x 11) of your favorite photos of trips, etc. Slip into clear covers
    (office supply store) and store in organized notebooks.

8. Keep modeling compound, wax sticks, glossaries and dictionaries
    readily available for Word Play activities.

EASY START WORD LISTS

Words that sound similar

quiet	quite	meet	meat
fair	fare	ever	every
plain	plane	to/too	two
trial	trail	rain	rein
whole	hole	which	witch
knew	new	by	buy
be	bee	bin	been
ball	bell	except	accept
know	no	son	sun
so	sew	see	scene
their	there	hour	our
sell	cell	close	clothes
lessen	lesson	pen	pin
weather	whether	sent/scent	cent

Interesting phrases (idioms)

all ears
back on his feet
dog-tired
big-shot
birds of a feather
blow off steam
bring home the bacon
by the skin of one's teeth
chew the fat
chin up
chips are down
cream of the crop
cry wolf
down to earth
elbow grease
face the music
fair and square
feel it in one's bones
fifty-fifty
fit as a fiddle

flash in the pan
fly in the ointment
foot the bill
for a song
forty winks
from A to Z
get on one's nerves
get the upper hand
get wind of
ghost of a chance
give the cold shoulder
go to bat for
have irons in the fire
in the nick of time
kill two birds with one stone
leg to stand on
like a fish out of water
make ends meet
nip in the bud
nose to the grindstone
on its last leg
on the dot
out of the question
put one's foot in one's mouth
put two and two together
right-hand man
rub someone the wrong way
save face
scare the daylights out of
see eye to eye
skate on thin ice
slip through one's fingers
stiff upper lip
strike while iron's hot
take the bull by the horns
turn over a new leaf
under the weather
win hands down

BASIC SIGHT WORD LIST

Here is a selected list of some of the most common words in English. You would find these in about one-half of all textual material, so practice. Notice the words are highly abstract; it makes sense to also teach a more concrete list of words taken directly from your environment.

Common suffixes: <u>ing, es, ly, er, ly, est, ed, er</u>

High frequency sight words:

a	for	not	something
at	far	now	sometimes
and	from	nothing	to
as	first	or	the
all	go	of	they
am	get	on	than
always	had	off	that
an	her	once	this
are	have	over	today
again	how	our	there
about	has	one	through
anything	he	often	their
by	him	out	these
be	help	other	then
big	I	probably	two
because	it	please	too
but	in	play	up
been	is	put	under
can	into	quiet	use
come	if	quite	very
could	its	run	was
do	just	read	will
did	let	red	we
does	like	ran	way
down	look	ready	who
eat	my	real	word
each	more	sit	would
enough	maybe	say	with
early	me	she	were
easy	must	see	which
even	many	so	what
every	make	some	when
everyone	most	said	while
enough	no	should	where

EASY START GLOSSARY

Chunking:
 Breaking new concepts (any learning sequence) down into individual pieces
Comprehension:
 Understanding text, getting meaning from print- the purpose for reading
Decoding:
 Unlocking or 'cracking' the written code; word analysis or recognition
Fluency:
 Automaticity, the instantaneous recognition of words
Guided reading:
 Teacher provides a structured reading experience, as directed reading activity
Look backs:
 Looking back into previously read material for a more accurate response
Miscues:
 Reading errors, responses which are different from actual text
Multi-sensory styles:
 Modalities: visual, auditory, tactile/ kinesthetic (muscle memory/ movement)
Phoneme:
 Smallest unit of sound, smaller than syllables; phonemic awareness
Phonics:
 Word recognition (code) by one- to- one sound/ symbol relationships
Reading strategy:
 Methods and activities planned to teach literacy skills
Scanning:
 Selectively quick reading of material, dipping in for specific information
Schema:
 (Schemata), prior knowledge; what is known before the reading is done
Sight words:
 Non- phonetic, generally abstract words which must be instantly recognized
Skimming:
 Fast reading to get overall meaning of textual material
Structural analysis:
 Recognizing roots, prefixes, suffixes, syllables, inflectional endings
Tracking:
 Following along a line of print, involves directionality and visual focus
Vocabulary:
 Knowledge of words and their meanings (reading and speaking vocabularies)

FAVORITES FROM '02 EDITION!
SELECTED RESOURCES
(Skill levels 1–12, and Adult)

BOOKS Time-Tested, oldies.

Brain Gym Teacher's Manual, related materials, training – www.braingym.com

Classroom Activities for Correcting Specific Reading Problems, Stephen A. Pavlak; Parker Pub. Co., 1985.

Dynamite Dictionary Skills, Jeri S. Cipriano, Good Apple, 1997.

Elementary Reading Strategies That Work, Davis & Lass; Allyn & Bacon, 1996.

Grammar Works! (Grades 4-8), (Reproducible Skills Lessons) Scholastic, 1996.

Graphic Organizers, K. Bromley, L. DeVitis, & M. Modlo, Scholastic.

Guided Reading, Good First Teaching For All Children, Mary Ellen Giacobbe; Heinemann, 1996.

Informal Tests For Diagnosing Specific Reading Problems, Stephen A. Pavlak; Parker Pub. Co., 1983.

Literacy at the Crossroads, Regie Routman; Heinemann, 1996.

Literacy Techniques For Successful Readers & Writers, Booth, Editor; Pembroke Pub., 1996.

Phonics, Too! How To Teach Skills In A Balanced Program, Wells, Hewins; Pembroke Pub., 1994.

Reading and Writing Remediation Kit, Wilma Miller; Center For Applied Research In Education, 1997.

Reading By The Colors, Helen Irlen; Avery Pub. Group, Inc., 1991.

Reading Workshop Survival Kit, Gray R. Muschla; Center For Applied Research In Education, 1997.

Smart Moves, Carla Hannaford; Great Ocean Press, 1995.

Spelling Smart! A Ready–To–Use Activities Program for Students with Spelling Difficulties, Cynthia M. Stowe; Center For Applied Research In Education, 1996.

Strategies for Reading Non-Fiction:Comprehension and Study Activities, Grades 4-8, Sandra Simmons; Spring Street Press, 1991.

Student Success Secrets, Eric Jensen; Barron's Education Series, 1996.

Teaching Grammar in Context, Constance Weaver, Boyton Cook Pub., 1996.

Teaching Students to Read Though Their Individual Learning Styles, Carbo, Dunn & Dunn; Allyn & Bacon, 1991.

Teaching Study Skills and Strategies in Grades 4 to 8, Mangrum, Ianuzzi, Strichart; Allyn & Bacon, 1998.

The Gift of Dyslexia, by Ronald D. Davis; Ability Workshop Press, 1994.

The Literature Teacher's Book Of Lists, Judie L. H. Stouf, Center For Applied Research In Education, 1993.

The Myth of the ADD Child, Thomas Armstrong; Penguin, 1995.

The Reading Teacher's Book Of Lists, Fry, Kress & Fountoukidis; Prentice Hall, 1993.

The Study Skills Handbook, Jay Amberg; GoodYear Books, Scott Foresman, 1993.

The Study Skills Handbook, (Grades 4-8), Judith Dodge, Scholastic Prof. Book, 1994.

Word Matters, Pinnell & Fountis, Heinemann, 1998.

SPEED READING

Breakthrough Rapid Reading, Peter Kump, Prentice Hall, 1979.

Power Reading, Laurie Rozakis, MacMillian.

Speed Reading, Tony Buzan, Penguin Books, 1991.

Super Reading Secrets, Howard Stephen Berg, Warner Books, 1992.

GETTING STARTED WITH NLP: (Creating Peak Performance Champions)—the study of excellence

Introducing NLP, Neuro Linguistic Programming; O'Connor & Seymour; Harper Collins Publisher, 1990.

MOTIVATIONAL FAVORITES

A Better Way to Live, Og Mandino, Bantam Books, 1990.

Awaken the Giant Within, Anthony Robbins, Fireside Books, 1991.

In Search of Excellence, Thomas Peters,Warner Books, 1992.

Maximum Achievement, Brian Tracy, Simon & Schuster, 1993.

Over the Top, Ziglar, Thomas Nelson Publishers, 1994.

The Master Motivator, Hansen & Batten, Health Communications, 1995.

Dr. Norman Vincent Peale's Books— ALL are great.

OTHER GREAT LITERACY TITLES:

Best Practices in Literacy Instruction, Various editors, Guilford Press, 1999.

Picture Me Reading, Marlys Isaacson, 2002. (800) 235-6822

Practicing What We Know (Informed Reading Instruction), Constance Weaver, Editor, NCTE, National Council Teachers of English, 1998, 800-369-6283.

Teaching Reading in the Content Areas, Billmeyer & Barton, McRel, 1998. (303) 337-0990.

Reading Champions!

Mrs. Rita Wirtz, M.A.

Bringing focus to reading instruction and
helping students master fundamental reading skills:
PHONEMIC AWARENESS
PHONICS
FLUENCY
VOCABULARY
TEXT COMPREHENSION

Research has identified the necessary skills for successful reading instruction. In the national ***Reading First Initiative***, five critical reading skills are identified. The first of these is *phonemic awareness*, which means recognizing and manipulating sounds in spoken words. The second skill is *phonics*, understanding the relationship between phonemes (sounds) and graphemes (letters) which represent the sounds. *Fluency* is the ability to read quickly and accurately and is related to automaticity. *Vocabulary* means knowing the meaning of words in order to effectively communicate. Finally, *comprehension* refers to deriving meaning from print.

Summary and sub-group reports by the National Reading Panel closely match most state Standards and Frameworks. The importance of evidence-based reading instruction forms the backbone of standards-driven curriculum. The ability to teach a balanced program of code and meaning, combined with effective strategic instruction cannot be overstated.

Reading Champions! strategies help teachers translate complex research into everyday classroom routine. These activities are not designed to take the place of other researched and quantified evidenced-based programs, but to offer teachers working tools to help schools and families extend learning. The activities and suggestions in ***Reading Champions!*** offer classroom teachers and teaching at home families ready-to-use lessons which were field tested and perfected in over five hundred classrooms and should be easily replicated. Second language learners and those with special needs benefit from the multitude of approaches offered.

Strong, Silver and Pernini in *Making Students as Important as Standards* (ASCD, Instructional Leadership, Nov. 2001) make a good case for double alignment, the notion that curriculum, instruction and assessment need to be aligned to both students and standards.

AFTERWORD

On Optimism:

As a cancer survivor, I can assure you that the only
thing that saved me was a small voice inside of me that suddenly started
screaming, "Life is worth the effort!"
I wanted to live for granddaughter Morgan's wedding.

Her little hands, smiling face and voice gave me strength when there was none.
Only my optimism remained during daunting times and a life beyond what I
could endure. My natural optimistic spirit shone through when there was nothing
left but hope and all gave up, even me. Find one thing today to focus on, see its
beauty, savor the energy and I promise you that commitment makes

the difference in a gracious life worth living, no matter what.

Rita Wirtz
October 12, 2018

About the Author

Rita Wirtz served as Title I ESEA Program Evaluator in the California Penal System, Curriculum Consultant for Sacramento County Office of Education, School Principal, Reading Instructor, K-Adult Teacher, and Special Needs Educator. She shared her experiences as Keynote Speaker and Seminar Leader traveling throughout the United States inspiring other educators and parents.

Mrs. Wirtz volunteered on numerous boards in Sacramento, California including Homeless Coalition, SARB (School Attendance and Review), Neighborhood Study Center, Fantasy Theatre, Harmony Arts, etc. She also volunteered for Homeschool groups, offering Keynotes and workshops on reading instruction.

Rita Keynoted for a multitude of organizations including school districts, California School Boards Association, Chapman University Commencements, Child Welfare and Attendance, Migrant education- Mini Corps, Kindergarten Conferences, Head Start, CASCD and ASCD, U.S. and international. (Supervision and Curriculum groups). Also, Mentor Teachers, Learning Disabilities Conferences, ECE (Early Childhood Education), Special Education SELPAs (service areas), etc.

Mrs. Wirtz holds a BA in English and Speech, Reading Specialist, Masters in Reading, and Administrative Services Credential, pre-Adult. Because of her work with speed reading, she also became a certified Hypnotherapist and NLP (Neurolinguistics) practitioner. Rita also studied Brain Gym.

Rita is devoted towards helping other instructors by sharing extensive life affirming experiences. Through her Housecalls', she provided demonstration lessons in nearly 600 classrooms, with all ages, preschool-adult. Walking the talk made her a sought after personality, with rave reviews at each appearance.

Besides teaching, her greatest love of all is writing. "Writing is like breathing." She has written a number of reading books for parents and teachers (including "Reading Champs: Teaching Reading Made Easy" published in 2014) and recently published her memoir about her life as a teacher, "Stories from a Teacher's Heart: Memories of Love, Life and Family". In addition, as Featured blogger on Bam! Internet Radio's Ed Words , Rita continues to bring fresh insights to the world of education and life. There are nearly 150 blogs for you to select from, on reading topics and everyday life.

Ms. Wirtz reflects on her accomplished career with humility and reflections of how all working toward common goals make a difference.

Other Writings by Rita M. Wirtz, MA

Teaching for Achieving: How to Get the Achievement Results You Want. 1995.

K-3 Reading Success! Finding the Balance (What Works—How to Do It). 1996.

The Very Best Classroom-Tested Reading Strategies Ever! (Reading Success Recipes from 500 Classrooms). 1999.

Reading Champions! Teaching Reading Made Easy. 2002.

Reading Champions! Teaching Reading Made Easy Video Set: Three Videos and Two Guidebooks. 2002.

50 Common Sense Reading Lessons (Reading success recipes for teachers, parents, classroom assistants and home schooling families). 2003.

Corrective Reading: Word Study. Reading Champions! Teaching Reading Made Easy (Steffen's Story), 2005.

Reading Champs, Teaching Reading Made Easy. LifeRich Publishing,, 2014.

"Letter to Michigan Moms Who Love Reading," Guest article for *Michigan Mom Living, Homeschool.* June, 2016.

"*Stories From a Teacher's Heart, Memories of Love, Life and Famil .y.* LifeRich Publishing, 2019. Featured Blogger, www.BAMRadioNetwork.com, currently nearing 150 blogs on EdWords, 2014-2021.

You can contactRita on her website: www.ritawirtz.com

blog: www.bamradionetwork.com/user/ritawirtz/

Instagram & Twitter: @RitaWirtz

Book Guide Introduction

by Rita Wirtz

Reading Champions! Teaching Reading Made Easy! reviews how to teach the fundamentals of reading, troubleshoot potential snags, and accelerate fluency, regardless of current reading levels. This book suggests how to teach some of the fundamental skills students need to meet state standards, and become capable confident readers who love to read!

Important keys to creating reading champions include:

1. Organize a print and language rich learning environment.
2. Crack the code with phonics fundamentals: vowels, consonants, compound words, contraction, syllables, prefixes and suffixes.
3. Practice spelling secrets that make a difference: patterns, rules, word families, prefixes and suffixes.
4. Boost word power with vocabulary builders and boosters.
5. Pick up the reading pace to remember and understand more material.
6. Use common sense comprehension and study skill techniques.
7. Master expository, non-fiction reading material.
8. Feature a "Novel a Month Club" to teach favorite core literature fiction.

Reading Champions! not only reviews the above topics, but puts the fun back into learning! This book makes teaching reading easier for busy teachers, tutors and parents. With its skill a day format, sctivities, chants, songs, games, graphic organizers and directed reading activities help promote fluent reading.
Best of all, these intervention strategies were successfully field tested in more than 500 K-12 classrooms, so you know everything works!

With today's emphasis on accountability, those of us teaching children to read or read better need every bit of available assistance. In order to beat the odds and ensure no child is left behind, it's necessary to rethink prevailing practices and add plenty of tools to the teaching toolbox. With the availability of information about what works to teach reading there is little reason for the achievement gap to continue. Yet too many children fall between the cracks and are left behind.

Reading Champions! helps you develop active, motivated and skillful readers. Moreover, its mini-lessons reflect research- based practices which are consistent with many state standards. The practical, ready- to- use strategies stand on their own. However, it is always interesting to compare notes with other teacher-researchers as we expand our own instructional repertoire. Reading *Champions!* is strategic, offering strategies for phonics, word study, fluency, vocabulary development, reading for information, reading fiction and studying. It reflects what <u>really works</u> in schools, in real-life classrooms.

The following guide was written by Kathleen Bulloch, a member of the Executive Board of the Califolnia ASCD (Association for Supervision and Cmriculum Development). It can be used for school-wide dialogue regarding best practices, discussion groups and individual reflection. I hope this document makes an important difference in your instructional success, with every becoming a great reader!

Chapter 1: Set the Stage to Create Success

1. What are the components of a balanced literacy program?
2. Describe the skills that should be included in a reading curriculum and give specific examples.
3. Share examples of language-rich classroom environments you have created in your classroom or school. Refer to print-rich list.
4. How are high interest reading materials incorporated in your school curriculum? Share specific examples.
5. According to the author, what formula is provided to motivate students to read? How should students be grouped when providing instruction?
6. Discuss the implications of the reading continuum for teaching and learning.
7. Have group members select a "Beat the Odds" idea and express their views/comments.

Chapter 2: Easy Start Lesson Planning

1. Discuss the process of a) lesson planning and b) skills teaching.
2. Review the warm up ideas, brain breaks and transitions. Discuss strategies you have used or will plan to use with your students to get their attention.
3. How can you assist students to follow directions more effectively?
4. Describe the use of "sets" and cite specific examples. What does "WIFM" stand for?
5. Why is it important to close your lesson with an appropriate strategy? Which activities have you used or plan to use?
6. What criteria need to be considered to get results with reading mini-lessons? What does "ME" stand for?

Chapter 3: Basic Reading Success Recipes

1. Review the reading process described in chapter 3. What are its implications for your instructional practices?
2. What are the major factors of reading?
3. Describe the visual and perceptual problems that may interfere with reading.

4. What role does directionality and tracking have on reading? What are some of the techniques teachers can utilize for these skills?
5. Discuss the basic skills to be mastered at the emergent and early reading levels.
6. Select a book. Describe how it can be used to teach basic reading skills.
7. Review the basic phonics information from chapter 3. How do you use phonics in your instruction? Provide samples to the group. How will you use the techniques presented in the book?
8. What is the role of word recognition skills in the development of reading? List the decoding sequence.
9. Select a new activity you will do with your students and report back to the group.

Chapter 4: Teach Structural Analysis

1. What are the components of structural analysis? What is its role in reading achievement?
2. Review the strategies and activities for teaching compound, prefixes and suffixes, syllables, and contractions. Use one of these activities with your students and report back to the group, bringing samples of student work. Share one of your own teacher designed activities for one of these skills and share with the group.
3. What strategies and techniques were most effective and why? What difficulties did students have in acquiring the above skills and why?

Chapter 5: Reading Shortcuts and Interventions

1. Describe and discuss the twelve common word recognition problems.
2. Brainstorm strategies for remediating each of the word recognition problems. Share samples from your own teaching.
3. Select an intervention/remediation activity from chapter 5 to use in your classroom. Report back to the group the results of the activity with student samples and other artifacts.
4. Review the multi-sensory literacy strategies. Discuss how you can incorporate some of the ideas in your classroom reading progra

Chapter 6: Word Slingers

1. Discuss the correlation between vocabulary knowledge and reading comprehension.
2. Share a vocabulary activity you use in your classroom with group members.
3. What rules do teachers need to know to help students spell new words correctly?
4. How can spelling be reinforced to specifically address the multiple intelligences?
5. What are the top ten spelling secrets, according to the author?

Chapter 7: How Reading Champions Read Non-Fiction

1. Why are some textbooks easier to read than others?
2. Critique the current textbooks you are using in your classroom. How "student-friendly" are they?
3. Describe the characteristics of a "Reading Champion" before, during and after reading experiences.
4. Share your teaching strategies for presenting reading skills to your students (word meaning skills, comprehension, and study skills).
5. What are some research-based techniques for improving reading rate and comprehension?
6. What is meant by "directed reading"? Cite some examples using content area textbooks.
7. Review the handouts in this section. Select one you will use and report back to the group. Describe how you have already used a similar technique.

Chapter 8: Easy Start Memory Joggers

1. What is the role of "memory joggers" and cite specific examples.
2. Review the memory techniques in chapter 8. Why is this knowledge important for teachers?

Chapter 9: How Reading Champions Read Fiction

1. What are the basic elements to include when teaching core literature classics?
2. Share student samples of book reports, book projects, and activities you have used in your classroom utilizing core literature.
3. Review the handouts in this section. Select one you will use in your class and report back to the group. Share one you have designed for your students.
4. How can teachers motivate students to read?

Culminating Activities

- Host a "Reading Champions" school event including reading demonstrations, student work samples, and student testimonials.
- Share samples of intervention strategies you have used from this book in your classroom or school.
- Consider sharing the reading lessons illustrating techniques taken from this book. Share with group members and critique.
- Invite students to your discussion group who have become "Reading Champions". Have students share their success stories. What techniques worked for them and why?

THE VERY LAST COMMENT

Reading skills improve with effort.

You need to motivate students to make the effort.

Rita Wirtz